3/29/89

I♥SEX

I (HATE)●SEX

I ♥ SEX
I HATE SEX

Graham & Lynne Jones

NEW ENGLISH LIBRARY

British Library Cataloguing in Publication Data

Jones, Lynne
  I love sex . . . I hate sex.
  1. Sex relations – Humour
  I. Title   II. Jones, Graham
  306.7'0207

  ISBN 0-450-48551-X

A New English Library Original Publication 1989

Published by New English Library,
a hardcover imprint of Hodder and Stoughton,
a division of Hodder and Stoughton Ltd,
Mill Road, Dunton Green, Sevenoaks, Kent TN13 2YA
Editorial Office: 47 Bedford Square, London WC1B 3DP

Photoset by Rowland Phototypesetting Ltd,
Bury St Edmunds, Suffolk

Printed in Great Britain by St Edmundsbury Press Ltd,
Bury St Edmunds, Suffolk

CONTENTS

ACKNOWLEDGEMENTS

The authors would like to thank the publishers of all Britain's national daily and Sunday newspapers, *Time*, *Newsweek* and assorted magazines, for providing the basic raw material for this volume; also the publishers of more than a hundred books. The main sources are listed in a separate bibliography. Anyone who has been inadvertently omitted from our source list is invited to contact the publishers for inclusion in subsequent editions.

We should add that in our classification of remarks, writings or asides of the famous under the headings 'I love sex' and 'I hate sex', it is the words themselves which determine the context. We are not in any case ascribing fixed views or commenting on the past or present lifestyle of any individual.

A LITTLE WORD IN YOUR EAR . . .

The question of sex . . . stands before the coming generation as the chief problem for solution.
Havelock Ellis, pioneer sexologist

If sexual intercourse, as poet Philip Larkin maintained, began in 1963 [(which was rather late for me)/between the end of the Chatterley ban/and the Beatles' first LP] then it can equally be said that it must have ended in 1984 [(only twenty-one years more)/between Reagan's re-election/ and condom ads galore.]

It is not easy now to recall the days of the 1960s, when all you needed was love rather than a packet of 'Mates'; when sex supermarkets sprang up like magic mushrooms in every town; when porn shops proliferated even more than bowling alleys; and when sixty-five per cent of debs had lost their virginity by Goodwood.

Sex went on to survive Vietnam, the Osmonds, and herpes, but could not have been prepared for such a trumpeted decline, the seal of which was set by *Time* magazine in Orwellian 1984 with a cover story proclaiming: 'SEX IN THE '80s – The Revolution is Over'. Letters poured in from the Blue Guards of the new cultural order: 'I am a 24-year-old male virgin and proud of it . . . We should concentrate on loving one another without attaching carnality to each relationship.' By 1988 *Time* had undermined sex's estab-

lished order of Kinsey and Masters and Johnson,
challenging the latter's shock-horror book on Aids as
well as the statistical basis for the third Hite report.
The office stationery cupboard (and the space behind
the filing cabinet) would never be the same again.

What 'killed' the sexual revolution was not just the
rapid spread of Aids (and all those anti-Aids ads) –
though this brought things into deathly focus – but
also the social change brought about by a new generation of young people who began to question, and
reject, the liberal values and hedonism of the laissez-
faire 1960s and 1970s. The 'me' generation didn't just
become the 'we' generation. They heeded the warning
signs, vacuumed up the condom culture, and got back
to earning money. Who needs LSD when you can go
for £sd? Who needs the big 'O' when you can go for the
big $?

By the mid-eighties, a new genre of book began to
appear which, even if it had made the publishers' lists
ten years before, would have been a certainty for mass
remaindering. Back to the nunnery and the Middle
Ages: *The New Celibacy; The Limits of Sex; Sex is not
Compulsory*. One wonders how long before instant
reversals of previous bestsellers begin to appear:
'Celibacy and the Single Girl'; 'The Joy of Non-Sex';
'Hollywood Eunuchs'; 'Not Having It At All'.

In a repudiation of Freud and the modern sex gurus,
the new books spelled out the joys of sexual frugality,
and, for the first time, began to look at the asset side of
the balance sheet: no Aids, no herpes, no cervical
cancer, no cystitis, no sexual diseases at all. No un-
wanted pregnancies. No embarrassing sudden heart
attacks. No dodging of jealous husbands and wives.
No falling prey to viruses due to fluctuating hormone
levels. No over-writhing and over-perspiring. Less

smoking and drinking, more *Match of the Day*. No traumas from complicated relationships. More TV darts. More TV snooker.

The balance-sheet aficionados will have already been chalking up their own score for 'liabilities': no fun, no intimacy, no body contact – no sleep. More *Match of the Day*, more TV darts, more TV snooker. The unconvinced will also by this stage be saying: 'sexual intercourse, *dead*?'

It can certainly be counter-argued that reports of the death of sex are a gross exaggeration. Just go to any maternity hospital or municipal park on a summer Saturday night, or tune into any TV channel after 10pm (well, at least after *News at Ten*). There were few events that captured the public admiration more than the allegation that Britain's highest paid businessman, Sir Ralph Halpern, managed to perform five times a night with leggy photographic model Miss Fiona Wright.

Sex – Who wants it? Who *needs* it? This book, with its mirror-image pages giving diametrically opposed viewpoints, is an attempt to set out the record of argument and let you, the reader, decide.

Some of the views you will read here are straightforward, others deep and meaningful. Some literary, some merely worldly wise. Some are witful, others wilful, though none, we hope, smutty or offensive. All are entertaining and together introduce a fresh element of fun into what has become, whatever the BMA, the Church Synod or Michael Jackson may say, the great debate of the day.

Barnet, Hertfordshire, 1988

Lynne Jones
Graham Jones

SEX – WHO WANTS IT?

We might as well make up our minds that chastity is
no more a virtue than malnutrition.

Dr Alex Comfort

So who wants sex? Well, one-time wisdom would
have been that we all do. Is it not the route to not only
bodily, but spiritual contentment? The key to tempor-
ary nirvana? The unison of souls that sets man as a
species apart from the rest?

I thought of losing my virginity as a career move.

Madonna

Sex is like a candy box. When it's open, why resist?

Mick Jagger

SEX – WHO *NEEDS* IT?

When I look across a crowded room at a girl I have to ask myself, is she worth dying for?

Aids-worried friend quoted by
Paula Yates

So who *needs* sex? Isn't it true that man and woman can live a truly fulfilled life without animal coupling rites? Isn't an abstinence from sex going to bring much calmer, healthier individuals free from disease and with above all, much more time to enjoy the *real* pleasures of life?

Sex is not compulsory. It's only a device, a kindly confidence trick perpetuated by Nature for purely functional reasons.

Jan Morris

Two-and-a-half minutes of squelching.

Johnny Rotten (It was alleged that
he later amended this to five
minutes because of a slightly more
energetic co-conspirator.)

Sex – Who Wants It?

The most fun I've had without laughing . . . Sex
between two people is wonderful, providing you can
get between the right two people – between five, it's
fantastic.

Woody Allen

Perhaps no human experience comes closer to a union
with universal consciousness than intercourse with a
loving other. It is the peak, the culmination of one of
life's most exciting, satisfying, and often awe-
inspiring gifts. And part of the gift of this experience is
orgasm – one of the most natural transitory endow-
ments we can claim – where we can shift from animal
to man to God.

Dr Irene Kassorla, Nice Girls
Do!

We play with the sexual side of the Lover-Shadow; we
relieve and drug the dissatisfaction of our imaginations in a purely sexual adventure, and suddenly sex
turns upon us and grips us. We slip off to the little
restaurant, the house of assignation; we creep up the
staircase and along the corridor; we hide together in
the thicket, and it is just to be a bright, almost momentary, flash of indulgence, and, before we know where
we are, the haunting deeper need to possess and be
possessed, for good and all, that undying hunger of
the soul for a commanding love-response, has laid
hold upon us.

H. G. Wells

Sex – Who Needs It?

Normal people don't enjoy talking about it.

Lana Turner

Relationships are not all about humping. We've been pressurised into thinking they are since the Pill. In the 1960s you saw someone you liked and jumped into bed with them. Three weeks later all their nasty habits came out.

Hazel O'Connor

Sexual intercourse is not intrinsically banal . . . It is intense, often desperate. The internal landscape is violent upheaval, a wild and ultimately cruel disregard of human individuality, a brazen, high-strung wanting that is absolute and imperishable, not attached to personality, no respecter of boundaries; ending not in sexual climax but in a human tragedy of failed relationships, vengeful bitterness in an aftermath of sexual heat, personality corroded by too much endurance of undesired, habitual intercourse, conflict, a wearing away of vitality in the numbness finally of habit or compulsion or the loneliness of separation. The experience of f——ing changes people, so that they are often lost to each other and slowly they are lost to human hope.

Andrea Dworkin, Intercourse

Sex – Who Wants It?

It is not news that sex for sex's sake can be fun.

Warren Beatty

I lost my virginity when I was 16 – to an 18-year-old high-school girl. She licked my earlobe. Nobody had licked my earlobe before. She said, 'It's time', and I said, 'I know.' She took me upstairs to her mother's bedroom. It was amazing. After that, I never looked back.

Eddie Murphy

James Thurber once asked the question, 'Is sex necessary?' My immediate answer is an unqualified *yes*. Women are undergoing a sexual renaissance. After centuries of guilt and repression, the bait of sexual pleasure has at long last been separated from the hook of reproduction. We finally have acquired sexual freedom. Women now have the opportunity to experience their full sexual potential, however and whenever they wish. For me, sex is a central force in life – an act of love, an act of godlike procreation, and an act of fun and recreation.

Dr Irene Kassorla

What does one want when one is engaged in the sexual act? That everything about you give its utter attention, think only of you, care only for you . . . every man wants to be a tyrant when he fornicates.

Marquis de Sade

Sex – Who Needs It?

It's better to have no sex than bad sex.

Ian Dury

Sex becomes much less important as you get older. Like most little girls I fell madly in love with horses, I was a stable groupie until I discovered boys. Then I had to cope with that from the age of 15 to 45 and now I have discovered gardening. It's a case of hormones being replaced by horticulture.

Audrey Eyton, leading dieteer

Disguising male lust has been essential to the ruse. In creating sadospiritual religion, men have fled into pseudo-purified and disguised lust In the Name of the Sublime. Phallic lust – christened *religion, mysticism, duty, charity, patriotism, romantic love* – is not only all right, but the height of the virile virtue. Indeed, male rape fantasies become high theology and elicit religious rapture when these are vaporised and condensed, elevated and converted, into dogma and art concerning the 'Virgin Birth'. In the 'Annunciation' the male-angel Gabriel brings poor Mary the news that she is to be impregnated by and with God. Like all rape victims in male myth she submits joyfully to this unspeakable degradation.

Mary Daly, Pure Lust

It is now technically possible to reproduce without the aid of males (or, for that matter, females) and to produce only females. We must begin immediately to do so. The male is a biological accident: the Y (male) gene is an incomplete X (female) gene, that is, has an incomplete set of chromosomes. In other words, the

Sex – Who Wants It?

Sex is like a smorgasbord – you should pick what you want.

Little Richard

After all, sexual pleasure, sex, orgasm, are obviously not things only men can give women. The body, without the mind's anxious censorship, is extremely liberated. It does not care what stimulates it, from its own hand to that Welsh music-hall sex object, the sheep . . . Long lists of begats in the Bible are capable of engendering a slight flush. Descriptions in school biology books of the mating habits of frogs I find distinctly erotic. Many quite ordinary farming practices have a certain sexy charm . . . Bondage, rude limericks, sadism, masochism, waterfalls, flakey bars, fantasies of rape – you name it and, at one time or another, I've been turned on by it.

Jill Tweedie, Guardian
*(in a critique attacking the
'sexlessness' of 'New' Lesbianism)*

Q. You'd never contemplate a life of celibacy even though they say it's good for the soul?
A. I'd rather commit suicide.

*Jimmy Somerville,
the Communards*

16

male is an incomplete female, a walking abortion, aborted at the gene state.

> *Valerie Solanis, excerpts from the*
> *SCUM (Society for Cutting Up*
> *Men) manifesto*

Bed is for sleeping on.

> *Elvis Presley*

The sex life of spiders is very interesting. He f——s her. She bites off his head.

> *Valerie Solanis,* Sisterhood is
> Powerful

"OH, HI ROBERT!"

Sex is something I really don't understand too hot. You never know where the hell you are.

> *J. D. Salinger,*
> Catcher in the Rye

ADVICE FROM THE
TOP . . .

What comes first in a relationship is lust – then more lust.

Jacqueline Bisset

So the issues have been spelt out. But what do world leaders/opinion formers/major figures have to say on the subject? For wholly public-spirited purposes, we have sought out the views of a brace of distinguished sexologists, assorted Hollywood wives, one former US presidential contender and two actual Presidents – plus, in case you were getting bored, Bill Wyman and Lord Longford.

People cannot eliminate sex from their lives altogether, even if they want to. Sex is a natural function. We can all control our natural functions for only a short time. We can hold our breath for a little while, or put off sleep or suppress a cough. But, eventually, time runs out on control of our natural functions. With sex we can control it only when we are awake.

Once we go to sleep, the natural function takes over. Every man in reasonably good health, regardless of age, has an erection every eighty to ninety minutes all night long, whether he is dreaming or not. Every reasonably healthy woman lubricates every eighty to ninety minutes during sleep.

ADVICE FROM THE TOP . . .

Is that all there is to it?

Prince Charles to lady confidante,
quoted by Daily Star *diarist Peter Tory*

Having cantered crisply round the course, it does not seem entirely advantageous to regale you with our own views on this important matter. So here instead are the opinions of an array of leading figures and official oracles, including the glorious founder of the Soviet Union, one US President, Charlie Nicholas and George Michael.

Sex – this theme has become a permanent one today for the press, radio and television of the bourgeois West.

The transformation of the most intimate relations into Public Topic Number One, and of the naked body into a major attraction for viewers and audiences, the general sexual atmosphere which creates the impression of general madness – all this impresses anyone who visits the capitalist countries today, the United States or Sweden, Britain or West Germany.

Literary Gazette,
a Soviet Union journal

Advice From The Top

So even those who believe they are completely celibate cannot control the natural sexual functions of their bodies.

Dr William Masters, US sexologist

Women who have really learned to enjoy sex are usually fascinated by their partner's apparatus . . . and learn to play with it fully and skilfully. Good hand and mouth work practically guarantee a good partner.

Dr Alex Comfort, The Joy of Sex

Sex is terrific – I wallow in it.

Linda Gray (Sue Ellen of Dallas)

I don't think it is possible to be monogamous these days . . . I don't know anyone who is faithful, or indeed, wants to be.

Jacqueline Bisset, 1976

Good girls go to heaven. Bad girls go everywhere.

Helen Gurley Brown, founder of Cosmopolitan

Letter to George Burns: 'Dear George, I've been married for eight years. I love my wife very much, but she's a nymphomaniac. What should I do?'
George Burns' reply: 'Stop writing letters and count your blessings.'

Sex is sometimes better without love – it's more exciting.

Kate O'Mara

"I FIND BOOKS M
ANYTHING

I used to be a terrible man for my nookie – but not any more. Why not? Because of Aids, you stupid girl, that's why not.

Robbie 'Tutti Frutti' Coltrane

The fruit you never had, you never miss. Some of the greatest writers in the world were celibate. I don't think that George Bernard Shaw, for instance, ever bothered Mrs Shaw very much.

Kenneth Williams

I find books more entertaining than anything, or anybody else.

Chaka Khan

NTERTAINING THAN
YBODY ELSE."

CHAKA KHAN

I got addicted to Pimms on my honeymoon. It's the only thing I got addicted to, mind!

Princess of Wales, as told to the
Sun *by Britannia steward Keith Jury*

I haven't made love on a Friday night for a few years now. I always avoid it. I want to be on peak performance for the match.

Charlie Nicholas

If you can combine sex and fun, that's great, but the earth has never moved for me.

George Michael

21

Advice From The Top

But, sir – you haven't seen any intercourse yet.

> *Manager of live sex-show*
> *protesting to Lord Longford*
> *during his fact-finding mission to*
> *Copenhagen. (Said His Lordship:*
> *'I was disgusted, but it is our*
> *duty to see such things.')*

Sex, treated properly, can be one of the most gorgeous things in the world.

> *Elizabeth Taylor*

I think it makes you tremendously creative. Every couple of days there is a new person with a new body, a new face, a new way of thinking – it inspires you in a different way.

> *Bill Wyman*

What a lovely way to spend a Saturday afternoon.

> *President John F. Kennedy on*
> *making love to Judith Campbell*
> *Exner, whom he shared with a*
> *Mafia boss*

Sex is an overwhelming emotion. I will say that if I feel the need to express any emotion I'm going to do it.

> *Dolly Parton*

Sex? It's best in the afternoon coming out of the shower.

> *Ronald Reagan, 1957, quoted by*
> *actress Viveca Linofors while they*
> *filmed* Nigh Unto Night

It is no crime not to enjoy sex. It doesn't mean you're frigid. If you're celibate, friendships can be developed. Friends can sometimes be a lot more help than lovers in times of need.

Denise Coffey, actress

These days I'm astounded by people's behaviour, particularly with the danger of Aids. When we were in Brussels for the Eurovision Song Contest, the hotel was full of hookers. People were picking them up and I thought 'What happened to common sense?'

Terry Wogan, Daily Mail

I'd rather win an Oscar than a pretty girl. One is permanent and the other is not.

Jack Nicholson

Alexandra Kollontai: I regard sex like a glass of water from which I drink when I am thirsty.
Lenin: But who wants to drink a glass of dirty water?

Any girl who comes into my bedroom is in for a bit of a shock, because I've turned it into a recording studio.

Gene Anthony Ray of 'Fame'

I liked it better when the actors kept their clothes on.

Ronald Reagan, aged 70

HISTORY SAYS 'YES'

Let the woman feel the act of love to her marrow;
Let the performance bring equal delight to the two.

Ovid

From the Bacchanalian excesses of the Romans to the wife-swapping 1970s, sex in history has always operated on two levels. Superficially, one can point to the highpoints of chastity – the days of chivalry, maidens fair and crusaders; the high days of the Vatican and the cult of the Virgin Mary; the Puritan era; and the reign of Queen Victoria and 'Victorian values'.

But beneath the surface of every era in which sex was 'officially' rejected, private sexual licentiousness parodied public purity. In 1171, the Abbot of St Augustine, Canterbury, was found to have seventeen illegitimate children in one village (though his score was beaten in 1274 by the Bishop of Liège who managed sixty-five). Victorians may have covered piano legs to curb sexual arousal, but down the road, 'temples of voluptuousness' (brothels) were packing in the clients.

Sexual repression has gone hand in hand in history with sexual abandon.

HISTORY SAYS 'NO'

The pleasure is momentary, the position ridiculous, and the expense damnable.

Lord Chesterfield

The tide of sexual abstinence in the western world has ebbed and flowed in history very much in line with the fortunes of organised religion. The strength of the early Christian message converted much of the world's moral values. The cult of the Virgin Mary and the pre-eminence of the Catholic church made celibacy a calling and a virtue, then the ascension of Protestantism with its ritualised self-denial elevated chastity to a secular pedestal.

At no time did history say 'no' to sex, of course, quite like the Victorian era, when sofas were banned as 'sex chairs', midwives delivered babies under shrouds, women bathed from protective 'machines' in twenty-yard cotton cocoons, books by male and female authors were separated on the bookshelves, and no polite person would dream of offering a lady a chicken 'leg' (the very word a crime). One Methodist minister in St Martin's Lane, London, even tied the legs of his cockerel together so the henhouse was free of sin on the Sabbath.

Some of these anti-sexual attitudes can be traced back to classical history, while many persist today.

History Says Yes

There is no greater nor keener pleasure than that of bodily love.

Plato

Rare are those who prefer virtue to the pleasures of sex.

Confucius

Chastity keeps holiday, while lust is always very much occupied.

Seneca

The only chaste woman is one who has not been asked.

Spanish proverb

In Gramaneri many young men enjoy a woman that may be married to one of them, either one after the other or at the same time. Thus one of them holds her, another enjoys her, a third uses her mouth, a fourth holds her middle part, and in this way they go on enjoying her several parts alternately.

Kama Sutra

So given are they to the lusts of the flesh that some are addicted to the vile depravity of sodomy not only with boys but also with men and horses. People caught in such obscene acts are not severely punished.

Duke Frederick of Holstein's
representative in Moscow, 1630,
on the Russians of the time

Count your chastity more precious than your life.

Aeschylus

Nothing is better than a celibate life.

Horace

Venereal pleasures above all debase a man's mind.

St Thomas Aquinas

I never married, and I wished my father never had.

Greek epigram

Lust requires for its consummation darkness, secrecy; and this not only when unlawful intercourse is desired, but even such fornication as the earthly city has legalised.

St Augustine

Any woman who shall impose upon, seduce and betray into matrimony any of His Majesty's subjects by virtue of scents, paints, cosmetic washes, artificial teeth, false hair, iron stays, hoops, high-heeled shoes, or bolstered hips, shall incur the penalty against witchcraft, and the marriage . . . shall be null and void.

Early English Act of Parliament

History Says Yes

Virtue in woman is often merely love of their reputation and their repose.

Le Rochefoucauld, Maximes,
1665

There are few good women who are not weary of their trade.

Le Rochefoucauld again

'Tis the established custom in Vienna for every lady to have two husbands, one that bears the name, and another that performs the duties.

Lady Mary Wortley Montagu,
letter to friend, 1716

I need several mistresses. If I had only one, she'd be dead inside eight days.

Alexander Dumas

I must have a woman or I will freeze and turn to stone.

Vincent Van Gogh

Five times that night did I put her through the manual exercise of love, and five times did she die away in the most ecstatic of enjoyments . . .

The Pearl, *1879*

Why . . . I have sought the strumpets which I have done, I cannot explain, nor the frame of mind which led me into lascivious vagaries and admirations, fancies and caprices . . .

Walter, My Secret Life, *1885*

Certainly, the best workes, and of greatest Merit for the Publike, have proceeded from the unmarried, or Childless Men.

Francis Bacon, Essays: Of
Marriage and Single Life, *1612*

Virginity is the life of the angels, the enamel of the soul.

Jeremy Taylor, 1650

I swear I will be faithful; I could be trusted with fifty virgins naked in a dark room.

Nelson to Emma, Lady Hamilton

Kissing don't last: cookery do!

George Meredith, The Ordeal of
Richard Feverel, *1859*

Be on your guard against the whole tribe of bad women.

Ludwig van Beethoven

Experience every day convinces me that much of the labour of mind, confusion of ideas, and inability to control the thoughts of which married men complain, arise from the sexual excesses they commit.

Sir John Acton, historian

Sensual indulgence, however guilty in its circumstances, however tragic in its results is, when accompanied by love, a sin according to nature, fornication is a sin against nature.

Westminster Review, 1851, on prostitution

History Says Yes

Ah, Anna, thou hast been tasting soup before it is
ready. – Yes, and I found a carrot in it.

> *Pregnant barrow girl to a relative,*
> *1875, quoted by Elizabeth Roberts,*
> An Oral History of Working
> Class Women 1890–1940

Adultery is the application of democracy to love.

> *H. L. Mencken, 1920*

Sexual pleasure, widely used and not abused, may
prove the stimulus and liberation of our finest and
most exalted activities.

> *Havelock Ellis, pioneer sexologist*

Promiscuity is not just man's natural instinct, it is also
his most reasonable instinct. I have picked an apple: I
found it good. I want another: nothing is more reasonable than to pick that too.

> *Henri de Montherlant*

The ability to make love frivolously is the chief charac-
teristic which distinguishes human beings from
beasts.

> *Heywood Brown, US 'Algonquin*
> *Round Table' author*

ONE WONDERS HOW TWO
ELF-RESPECTING PEOPLE
OULD FACE EACH OTHER
FTER PERFORMING IT."
        W.T. STEAD

History Says No

Dear Ta-ra-ra: It surprises me to find that a girl sufficiently educated to write and spell well should be so deplorably ignorant of the common rules of society to think she may go out alone with a young man in his canoe. And furthermore, one whom she 'only knows slightly'.

Reply to reader from Girl's Own
Paper, *1895*

Sex is an act which on sober reflection one recalls with repugnance, and in more elevated mood even with disgust.

*Schopenhauer, German
philosopher*

It is monstrously indecent. One wonders how two self-respecting people could face each other after performing it.

W. T. Stead

A man marries to have a home, but also because he doesn't want to be bothered with sex and all that sort of thing.

Somerset Maugham

I don't see so much of Alfred any more since he got so interested in sex.

*Mrs Alfred Kinsey on her
sex-report pioneer husband*

31

THE BEST CURE FOR BACKACHE

I think I made his back feel better.
Marilyn Monroe after private
meeting with J. F. Kennedy

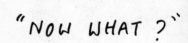

"NOW WHAT?"

Sex has its advantages, of course, such as providing something to do between 7.30 p.m. and 9.00 p.m. when television is awash with dreary quiz shows and husband-and-wife sitcoms. It can make you feel like a film star in your own bedroom – film stars, apparently, doing little else. It is still just about the only way to have babies (especially if you want them) and, well, doesn't it make your hair/toes/nose curl, and help you see in the dark?

Some reasons why sex is good for you:

IT'S A PAIN IN THE NECK

I've tried several varieties of sex. The conventional position makes me claustrophobic. And the others either give me a stiff neck or lockjaw.

Tallulah Bankhead

Sex has its disadvantages, of course, such as the implicit danger of an untimely kick on the handbrake from the rear seat of a Vauxhall Astra. It can bring cardiac arrest at home and police arrest when done in public. It can (and does) lead to babies (especially if you don't want them) and often necessitates an embarrassing visit to the chemists (er, pardon, Miss . . . have you got two gallons of baby lotion?).

Some reasons why sex is bad for you:

The Best Cure For Backache

It's healthy

Coition is one of the causes of the preservation of health. Let him among you, who is in a condition for having sufficient copulation, marry.

Mohammed

It keeps you young

I stay slim and young-looking because I love so much. And sex is important – without it you are dead. There is nothing worse than being sexually frustrated.

Ursula Andress, Revue *magazine*

It helps you relax

I don't usually get home before midnight. My wife and I have a tumble on the sofa and then I feel much better.

Phil Collins, 'Bizarre', the Sun

It's unhealthy

It is this constant abuse of the sexual organs, producing constant failures and the most loathsome diseases; it is this ridiculous force of a strong man putting forth all the nervous energy of his system, till he is perfectly prostrated by the effort, without one worthy motive, purpose or end; it is this which has so disgraced the act of impregnation . . . we must stop this waste through the sexual organs, if we would have health and strength of body.

Mrs Elizabeth Osgood Goodrich
Willard, Victorian social theorist
who believed sexual orgasm was
more debilitating to the system
than a whole day's work, 1867

It can give you nasty diseases

The cures were generally worse than the treatment. One doctor gave me a huge shot of penicillin up my arse after I got a dose of something. That night, I could hardly walk straight, I was wobbling all over the place. They practically had to carry me on stage with the band.

Ozzy Osborne

It's time-consuming

The only thing about being in love is that it takes up so much time.

Yoko Ono

The Best Cure For Backache

It's good exercise

I make love as much as possible because that is the best exercise of all (. . . though I still have to take a five-minute jog around the woods of Paris every morning).

> *Gerard Dimiglio, French star of*
> *'Emmanuelle 4',* You *magazine*

It helps you get to sleep

Lovemaking is the best sleep-inducer I know. Just like any woman, I have to get my beauty sleep. Getting enough rest is terribly important.

> *Sophia Loren,* Revue *magazine*

It's an intellectual stimulus

Sex alleviates the tension caused by love.

> *Woody Allen,* Daily Mail

It's good for business

I don't want to hear sweet nothings between the sheets – I want to hear sweet somethings – somethings I can use.

> *Aristotle Onassis on taking one particularly*
> *plain (but well-connected) companion – the*
> *wife of a shipping rival – quoted by*
> *biographer Peter Evans*

It can advance one's prospects

I don't advise people to sleep with someone simply to advance their social climbing career, but if they can love them at the same time, then it is very convenient.

> *Viviane Ventura, in advice to others,* Sunday *magazine*
> *(with a note of warning: 'Promiscuity is very*
> *damaging. It gets you the wrong reputation')*

"I'VE ALWAYS BEEN A FIRM BELIEVER IN MIXING BUSINESS WITH PLEASURE MISS PERRETT."

It can give you heart attacks
There is no human activity, eating, drinking, sleeping or sex, which some doctor won't discover leads directly to cardiac arrest.

John Mortimer, QC

It can be physically dangerous
Sex got me into trouble from the age of 15. I'm hoping that by the time I'm 70 I'll straighten out.

Harold Robbins

It's an intellectual drain
Painting and f——ing are not compatible. It weakens the brain.

Vincent Van Gogh

It's bad for business
Sex and business don't mix.

Bob Guccione, Penthouse *boss*

It can ruin one's prospects
It's hard enough for a woman to get ahead in this business without waking up in a different bed each morning.

New York TV presenter, anonymous
member of the NY Celibacy Club,
quoted by Time *magazine*

The Best Cure For Backache

Nice guys come last

I've made love the night before some of my biggest victories, and even the morning before an afternoon race.

Barry Sheene, Daily Express

If people are sensible, making love does improve your sporting performance. People get a better night's sleep after sex and this must be a help in the competitive strain next day.

John Sherwood, England
Commonwealth Games gold medal hurdler

You won't need a detox unit

I can never resist girls. It's worse than tea. I do have that problem, but it's a very healthy addiction, because you can't overdose on it.

Bill Wyman, Rolling Stone

It's peaceful

If the whole world dropped its pants – who could make war then?

Yoko Ono

It's a knockout

Of course a player can have sexual intercourse before a match and have a blinder. But if he did it for six months he'd be an old, decrepit man. It takes the strength away from the body.

Bill Shankly, Evening News

I aim to keep my fighters away from wives for three weeks before a fight. I bet they don't but I try. If you've made love the night before and get hit in the ring it's 'Goodnight all,' isn't it? If you've had two or three love sessions within forty-eight hours of a fight and get into the ring, you're like a dead body.

Freddie Hill, British boxing
trainer

It can be physically impossible

They say 'All the World Loves a Lover,' but what rot! During the past month, my girlfriend and I have been insulted and chased away from three shop doorways, three front gardens and four draughty alleyways.

Letter in Weekend, *quoted by the*
New Statesman's *'This England' column*

It's disruptive

Sex is a bad thing. It rumples the clothes.

Jacqueline Onassis attributed by
Gore Vidal, quoted by Peter York,
Style Wars (*via Jonathan Green*)

(Editor's note: It's very bad for new hairdos, and can even raise your golf handicap, too.)

THREE ALL-TIME
GREATS

GIACOMO CASANOVA (1725–1798)
No anthology of sexual behaviour could be complete
without a tribute to the Italian Lothario and adven-
turer whose name became synonymous with that of
the amoral, all-seducing libertine. Latin translator,
magician, gambler, ecclesiastical writer, soldier and
spy if not tinker and tailor, Giacomo Casanova set
standards of sexual wantonness and abandon few
could ever match.

The son of a promiscuous Venetian actress, the
young Casanova, after being expelled as a young man
from the seminary of St Cyprian for scandalous
conduct, embarked on a career of sexual conquest
breathtaking in its scope. 'There is not a woman in
the world who cannot resist constant attention,'
he wrote in advice to generations of would-be imita-
tors.

He was not merely a chauvinist of the 'love 'em and
leave 'em' fraternity we know so well. Casanova was a
sophisticated, sensual, sexual connoisseur, much re-
membered for his simultaneous seduction of the two
sisters Nanetta and Marta. He was also an incurable
romantic. If rebuffed, his ardour would only multiply.
He entrapped nuns, mothers superior and aristocratic
ladies but his true loves were teenage girls in the full
bloom of youth. He saw himself as a slave, not of lust,
but of love. 'I was all my life a victim of my senses. I
have delighted in going astray and I have constantly
lived in error, with no consolation than that of know-

THREE ALL-TIME GREATS

JOHN RUSKIN (1819–1900)

As the chief influence in bringing the Gothic revival to British architecture, he was the most important exponent of Victorian values of his day. It is fitting, therefore, that John Ruskin was the man behind the most public rejection of marital sex in recent history.

The son of a leading wine merchant, he had been betrothed at the age of 16 to the daughter of his father's Spanish partner, Adéle Domecq. But her Catholicism proved a stumbling block to the match.

He found instead a Scottish cousin of exquisite beauty, Euphemia ('Effie') Chalmers Gray, whom he married with due ceremony in 1848. What transpired on the wedding night after traditional nervous excitement has fascinated biographers to this day.

'Effie' found that her husband was unwilling to have sex, a matter he explained with every ounce of intellectual and literary argument that he could muster from his time at Christ Church, Oxford, where he had won the Newdigate prize for poetry (he later became the university's first Slade Professor of Art).

He cited religious precedent. He was, he said, imbued by the tradition of Christian chastity. He wished to preserve her considerable natural beauty from the ravages of depravity, not to mention pregnancy. He said he would consummate the marriage when she reached the age of 25.

When they both became leading members of the pre-Raphaelite social whirl, she found solace in the

ing I had erred.' Although tired and (understandably) worn out by the age of 40, he was proud of his achievements as a sexual athlete, constantly referring to his prowess in 'running the sixth race'.

He was constantly one step ahead of the law, not like de Sade as a consequence of debauchery, but rather from his gambling and financial excesses, though his dabbling in mysticism, freemasonry and magic did not make him popular.

His proud boast, at the age of 72, in his vivid and erotic autobiography was 'vixi' ('I have lived'). He was coy about his reputation. He had, he explained, 'an inclination to make new acquaintances, as well as a readiness to break them off.'

DORA RUSSELL (1894–1986)

A sexual pioneer breathtakingly ahead of her times in the 1920s, Dora Russell, second wife of the 'laughing' British philosopher, set an agenda for sexual liberation that was only substantially built upon in the 1960s and 1970s.

A leading socialist, suffragette and fellow of Girton, the young Dora Black had met the agonising free love advocate Bertrand Russell in 1919 and, in the same year, collaborating on book projects, they went to China together. She returned with him, eight months pregnant, and they married for the sake of legitimising the child.

Hers was a stronger will than his, as she embarked upon new ideas for mass sex education (including removing the stigma from masturbation) and set about in the courts challenging barriers to the promotion of condoms. As she saw it: 'We were trying to set sex free from the stigma of sin, we saw it as an expression of the union and harmony of two lovers.'

arms of John Everett Millais, and her virginity became the central feature of a famous legal battle for annulment.

She was later to have eight children. Ruskin, on the other hand, found himself at the mercy of a craving for pre-pubescent artistic models.

Some biographers cite Ruskin's stated aversion for female pubic hair as the reason for his attitude to marital sex. But more avowed students of Victoriana believe that his alleged impotence was the distillation of the anti-sex *mores* of the times.

Another eminent literary Victorian, Charles Kingsley, whose own marriage was not consummated for five uneasy weeks, wrote to his fiancée Frances Grenfell:' You do not know how often a man is struck powerless in body and mind on his wedding night.'

HARRIET MILL (1807–1879)

Those who believe that a platonic, non-sexual, man – woman relationship cannot endure need look no further than the case of Utalitarian guru John Stuart Mill and his wife Harriet Hardy for stultifying reproof.

Ms Hardy had dutifully married John Taylor, the prosperous junior partner in a wholesale druggists, in 1826. He was ten years older than her and she bore him three children. But the intellectual feminist burned quietly within her, and tired of him forcing his conjugal rights upon her in something approaching marital rape, she sought the advice of her priest.

He was William Johnson Fox, also an intellectual spirit. Unitarian minister and author of the *Monthly Repository*, he offered to introduce her to a polemicist who might sympathise with her predicament. John Stuart Mill was 24 and she was just 23. They met at a

Three All-Time Greats

Theirs was the definitive 'open marriage'. She attended the first World Sex Congress in 1926 (meeting the first two 'sex change' humans), insisting that she and Bertrand had no rights on each other's bodies. 'No man or woman has any right to invoke legal, moral, or religious sanction to compel another into sexual intercourse. No compulsion should here be recognised except the awakening of answering desire.' She signed up on the spot as English secretary of the World League for Sex Reform.

After her second child was born, the Russells set up the *avant-garde* Beacon Hill School which promoted free love among its staff. While her husband took advantage of this by having relationships with women teachers, she had embarked on an affair with American journalist, Griffin Barry, and bore him two children.

She said: 'There are no instincts less harmful or more productive in delight in the whole range of human interest and emotion than the desire for sex and love and the desire for children.'

But she bore the burden of promoting sexual liberation better than Bertrand: 'Bertie's severe Victorian upbringing and the intensity of his intellectual concentration had inhibited him sexually.' The ideas of free love drew them apart and their strained if revolutionary marriage ended in 1935.

JOHN F. KENNEDY (1917–1963)

'The Kennedy Administration will be known for its screwing the way the Eisenhower Administration was known for its golf,' predicted one White House aide when Camelot's foundations were first laid on Pennsylvania Avenue. When he heard this, according to

dinner party and their relationship was to last for 40 years.

The affair came to a head. Having told John Taylor she hated him, Harriet was told to renounce Mill and was packed off to Paris in order to forget him. Her husband had maintained a dignified silence as Mill became a more frequent visitor to the marital home, but had told her he could take no more. Mill broke a longstanding promise to his friend, Thomas Carlyle, and joined her in Paris, adopting the role of her platonic lover.

John Taylor died in 1849 and two years later, after the then conventional period of mourning, Harriet became Mrs John Stuart Mill, beginning a stabilised, asexual, if totally romantic marriage. Critics claimed that Mill had become 'in a state of subjection' to Harriet and this did raise questions as to the stability of their bond. She read and approved, for example, the extraordinary passages in his autobiography praising her as superior to himself intellectually, emotionally, and aesthetically.

Mill's words, however, remain as a treatise to the wisdom of platonic love. Their relationship, he said, was 'an edifying picture for those who cannot conceive friendship but in sex – nor believe that expediency and the consideration for the feelings of others can conquer sexuality.'

Mill's manifesto for celibate marriage tells how: 'We disdained, as every person not a slave of his animal appetites must do, the abject notion that the strongest and tenderest friendship cannot exist between a man and a woman without sensual relation, or that any impulses of that lower character cannot be put aside when regard for the feelings of others, or even when only prudence and personal dignity require it . . . We

Three All-Time Greats

one biographer, the President quipped: 'You mean nineteen holes in one day?'

John F. Kennedy allegedly not so much had it all as had them all. He was handsome. Charming. Warm. Courteous. Friendly. And above all, powerful. They flocked to him in droves – showgirls, models, secretaries – and he eagerly took the lead. 'No one was off limits,' his congressional friend, George Smathers told author Ralph G. Martino. 'Not your wife, your mother, your sister . . .' 'Sex to Jack Kennedy was like another cup of coffee, or maybe dessert,' said reporter Nancy Dickerson.

Known in the US navy as 'Shafty', JFK had an early brush with danger, becoming entangled with a Danish journalist suspected of being a Nazi spy. Setting out subsequently to cement his reputation as a sexual athlete, he began to collect sexual scalps like trading stamps. He told US Ambassador Clare Booth Luce he couldn't sleep without sex. He told British Premier Harold Macmillan a day without sex gave him headaches. 'Travelling with him was like travelling with a bull,' said old room-mate Smathers.

His two most legendary liaisons were with actress Marilyn Monroe and Judith Campbell Exner, whom he inconveniently shared with a top Mafia boss. In the meantime, while the world's press stayed dutifully silent, he was reportedly smuggling girls in and out of the White House, and sneaking into and out of ladies rooms and cupboards.

No one who knew of his escapades seemed to mind much. Many hundreds of women would back the standard defence of the Don Juan of modern power-politics, rationalised by actress Shirley MacLaine: 'I would rather have a President who does it to a woman than a President who does it to the country.'

did not feel under an obligation of sacrificing that intimate friendship and frequent companionship which was the chief good of life and the principal object in it, to me and I may also say to her.'

ANDY WARHOL

Asked to describe his favourite sex partner, he replied: 'My dog.' Two people kissing, he observed, always looked like fish. Anyone who *insisted* on having sex, he proclaimed, should stop doing it at 22. After then they were old, and looked ugly doing it.

Surrealist images from the most surrealist guru of celibacy, artist Andy Warhol, who found love in the lips of Marilyn Monroe but really, one supposes, had deeper erotic feelings for that Campbell's soup can.

'Sex is more exciting on the screen and between the pages than between the sheets anyway. Let the kids read about it and look forward to it, and then right before they're going to get the reality, break the news to them that they've already had the most exciting part, that it's behind them already.'

Love and sex, he observed, could go together and sex and unlove could go together, and love and unsex could go together. But personal love and personal sex were bad. His ideal wife, he observed, would have a lot of bacon, bring it all home, and own a TV station besides.

'I'd rather laugh in bed than do it. Get under the covers and crack jokes, I guess, is the best way. "How am I doing? Fine, that was very funny. Wow, you were really funny tonight."' If he went to a prostitute, he said, he would no doubt pay her to tell him jokes.

'A movie producer friend of mine hit on something when he said: "Frigid people can really make out." He's right. They really can and they really do.'

THERE IS NO ALTERNATIVE . . .

I never think about anything else. It is a religion.
Woody Allen

The words of the old joke just about sum it up: 'What's the difference between sex and an egg.' 'You can beat an egg . . .' To some people, sex is tops. The best in human experience. There is simply no alternative.

I think sex is the most interesting thing in the whole world. There's nothing like it and nothing is quite so good. It's the thing that occupies my mind more than anything else, and I would like it to occupy my time as much as possible.
Lesley Anne Down, Sunday magazine

My husband and I do it three or four times a night. I've always loved sex. I think I'm just a very horny bird.
Marti Caine

I am not a courtesan or a promiscuous woman, but I need to love and to be loved. My work, my whole way of being, cannot function without emotional nourishment.

Britt Ekland, True Britt

48

THERE ARE BETTER THINGS IN LIFE . . .

I'd rather have a cup of tea and a good conversation.
Boy George

It isn't the number one in life to many people. In fact a quick look at celebrity sayings of the moment may convince you that there are better things in life . . . Well, like cricket, snooker, sourdough . . .

Quite a lot of the time I prefer scrambled eggs to sex.
Eva Gabor

What I really love is to sit at home and watch my videos with my cigarettes, a little cake and a bag of sweets. I've even bought a video game and I play with that all night long.

Brigitte Nielson, ex-wife of Sylvester Stallone

I'm still a virgin and I can't see that changing. There are a lot more interesting things in life – gardening, for instance, or reading.

Jean Alexander, 'Hilda Ogden' of Coronation Street

49

There Is No Alternative

I've always found sex exciting.

Mick Jagger

Sex and horses: who can ask for more?

Sunday Telegraph, *reviewing*
Jilly Cooper's book Riders

Sexuality is only going to improve by the emphasis on pleasure. Women used to have the idea that to like sex is to be an evil woman or a nymphomaniac. Now they are getting the message that to be sexual is not to be unvirtuous. In the eighties it will manifest itself by women being able to tell their men what they want sexually.

Gay Talese, US writer

Sex is my favourite high these days. Better than any drug.

Peter Fonda

Sex to me is like football. I do it for the fun of it and then forget all about it.

John Taylor of Duran Duran

There Are Better Things In Life

If you cannot find love with a man or woman then find it in house plants, find it in creativity. It won't be the same thing but when you go to bed at night you may be less disappointed.

Tina Turner

I don't care about sex any more. It's years since I last made love. Nowadays, I so much prefer motorcycles.
Mickey Rourke

When I can't play cricket, I subordinate my desire with sex.

Anonymous public school
headmaster quoted in
The Guardian, 1973

If I had to choose between snooker and sex, then I would say snooker – because it's my life. It's what I've striven for, to be the best in the world. All right, you get a brilliant feeling when you have sex, but you also have a fantastic feeling when you play snooker – and it lasts. It goes on for weeks if you win the world championship.

Steve Davis

Frankly, after six or seven hours looking through a lens at every aspect of a girl's body, all I want to do is go home and watch football.

Adam Cole, photographer for Paul
Raymond's Club International

There Is No Alternative

I liked the boys and the boys liked me. I think men are exciting, and the gal who denies that men are exciting is either a lady with no corpuscles or a statue.

Lana Turner

I've always had an appetite for sex. To me, sex is just a way of having fun and excitement – and it doesn't cost as much as lots of other exciting activities.

33-year-old divorced woman
quoted by Masters and Johnson

I eat lots of spinach. It's good for making love. One must make love every day – it's good for your health and interior peace.

Lauren Hutton, Daily Mail

For most people, sex is just a need. I wouldn't give you tuppence for a male virgin.

Honor Blackman

I love men and I love sex. Sex is the one place where I feel safe, where I feel I can get it together with men.

Margot Kidder, girlfriend of Superman

Sex is my way of releasing tension. When you've been trying to drum up business all day and dealing with customers with a big smile, the tension builds up inside. At night I let it out with sex instead of getting bombed. And there are lots of gals around who are happy to hop into bed with me in return for dinner or a show.

32-year-old male stockbroker,
quoted by Masters and Johnson

There Are Better Things In Life

Sleeping with someone isn't the be-all and end-all of life. I'd rather have a guy take me to a football match and have a drink afterwards than go to bed with someone.

Samantha Fox

When it's a choice between food and sex, food will win all the time.

Shelley Winters

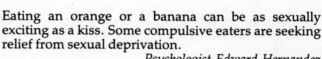

Eating an orange or a banana can be as sexually exciting as a kiss. Some compulsive eaters are seeking relief from sexual deprivation.

Psychologist Edward Hernandez
quoted in the Daily Mirror

You know sourdough is very sexy. When ever I don't have a girl I order a dozen a day.

Dustin Hoffman

HICH FILTHY PERSON HAS
ICKED ALL THE FRUIT ?"

Sex has never been an obsession with me. It's just like eating a bag of crisps. Quite nice, but nothing marvellous.

Boy George

Men have two basic needs in life, and neither – no matter what they say – is sex. They need love and work. The work takes priority over love. If a woman can know only one fact about men it should be that work is the most seductive mistress most men ever have.

Joyce Brothers, US psychologist

There Is No Alternative

Some people collect stamps. I collect crumpet.

Kenny Lynch, singer

Relatively few single, never-married adults seem to want to be sexually inexperienced.

Masters and Johnson, Crisis

There Are Better Things In Life

I can't understand any man seeing a woman purely for sex. I mean, if you can't talk politics with her afterwards – or before for that matter – what's the point of the relationship?

Ken Livingstone, MP

All this fuss about sleeping together. For physical pleasure I'd sooner go to my dentist any day.

Evelyn Waugh, Vile Bodies

A LITERATE VIEW

Sexual intercourse is like bicycle racing – the more you do it, the better you get at it.

Ernest Hemingway

'I must have women. There is nothing unbends the mind like them,' said John Gay in *The Beggar's Opera*. 'A woman's chastity consists, like an onion, of a number of coats,' Nathaniel Hawthorne unveiled as a universal truth in his Victorian *Journals*. 'Marriage may often be a stormy lake, but celibacy is almost always a muddy horse-pond,' wrote Thomas Love Peacock.

Literature, the physical distillation of man's spirit and imagination, has ever been on the side of full sexual fulfilment – the creative expression of procreative desire.

> Do you pine for a sweet night of love,
> For kisses without stop?
> Then let's embrace and let us go
> To bed, to bed, to bed.
>
> *Aristophanes*, Ecclesiazusae

A LITERATE VIEW

The universal preoccupation with sex has become a nuisance.

F. Scott Fitzgerald

'Man survives earthquakes, epidemics, the horrors of war, and all the agonies of the soul,' said Tolstoy, 'but the tragedy that has always tormented him, and always will, is the tragedy of the bedroom.'

'Sex is,' wrote Gore Vidal. 'There is nothing more to be done about it. Sex builds no roads, writes no novels and sex certainly gives no meaning to anything in life but itself.'

The agonies of the soul experienced by writers and poets through the centuries on the matter have led them to answers tortuous, tortured, and often in outright rejection of the deed:

Filth and old age, I'm sure you will agree
Are powerful wardens upon chastity.
Chaucer, Canterbury Tales

A Literate View

It is not politic in the commonwealth of nature to preserve virginity.

Shakespeare, All's Well That
Ends Well

I will find you twenty lascivious turtles ere one chaste man.

Shakespeare,
Merry Wives of Windsor

Marriage has many powers, but celibacy has no pleasures.

Samuel Johnson, 1784

A man has missed something if he has never woken up in an anonymous bed beside a face he'll never see again, and if he has never left a brothel at dawn feeling like jumping off a bridge into the river out of sheer physical disgust with life.

Gustave Flaubert

By Gis and by Saint Charity,
  Alack, and fie for shame!
Young men will do't, if they come to't;
  By cock, they are to blame.
Quoth she, before you tumbled me,
  You promised me to wed.
He answers:
So would I ha' done, by yonder sun,
  An thou hadst not come to my bed.

Shakespeare, Hamlet

That other burning which is but as it were the venom of a lusty and overabounding concoction, strict life and labour, which abatement of a full diet, may keep that low and obedient enough.

John Milton

I had a horror of prostitutes which never left me, and I could not look on a debauchee without contempt and even fear. Such had been my horror of immorality, ever since the day when, on my way to Petit Saconex along the sunken road, I saw the holes in the earth on either side where I was told such people performed their fornications. When I thought of this I was always reminded of the coupling of dogs, and my stomach turned over at the very thought.

Rousseau, Confessions

I am inclined to think that I have been less obsessed by these desires and imaginations than the average man. Occasional love reveries, acute storms of desire, are in the make-up of everyone. But in my case they have never dominated my scientific curiosities, my politico-social urge, or my sense of obligation.

H. G. Wells

A Literate View

Fifteen arms went round her waist.
(And then men ask: Are Barmaids chaste?)
John Masefield,
The Everlasting Mercy

I want to teach youths how to use their machine gun of
sex so that it may last for years, and when they come to
the double-barrel, how to take such care that the good
weapon will do them liege service right into their
fifties, and the single-barrel will then give them pleasure up to three score years and ten.
Frank Harris,
My Life and Loves

And I hope to spend eternity,
With my face buried beneath her breasts.
D. H. Lawrence (to paramour
Frieda Weeley)

I have been so misused by chaste men with one
wife,
That I would live with satyrs all my life.
Anna Wickham, Ship Near Shook

Every maiden's weak and willin'
When she meets the proper villain.
Clarence Day, Thoughts
Without Words

I keep making up these sex rules for myself, then I
break them right away.
J. D. Salinger, Catcher in the Rye

When you put a man and woman together, there are some things they simply have to do. They embrace. They warm each other. All the rest is dead and empty.

Ugo Betti, The Inquiry

I make time for sex between pictures or when I am bored.

Charles Chaplin

It is all this cold-hearted f——ing that is death and idiocy.

D. H. Lawrence,
Lady Chatterley's Lover

Tiffany Thayer is beyond question a writer of power: And his power lies in his ability to make sex so thoroughly, graphically, and aggressively unattractive that one is fairly shaken to ponder how little one has been missing.

Dorothy Parker

Accursed from birth they be/who seek to find monogamy/Pursuing it from bed to bed/I think they would be better dead.

Dorothy Parker again

Intercourse counterfeits masturbation.

Jean-Paul Sartre

A Literate View

Chastity – the most unnatural of the sexual perversions.

Aldous Huxley

I was a beautiful little boy . . . everyone had me – men, women, dogs, and fire hydrants. I did it with everybody. I didn't slow down until I was nineteen.

Truman Capote

Sex is one of the nine reasons for reincarnation . . . The other eight are unimportant.

Henry Miller

A Literate View

Sex is, so the cynics say, the last perversion. And the clerics of the Church of Rome are a living witness to the possibility of living with that perversion.

Anthony Burgess

No more about sex, it's too boring . . . poor honest sex, like dying, should be a private matter.

Lawrence Durrell, Tunc

I thought if this is how true love ends I'm glad I never had the experience.

Edna O'Brien,
Girls in their Married Bliss

RELIGIOUS VALUES

The Christian view of sex is that it is, indeed, a form of Holy Communion.

John Robinson, Bishop of
Woolwich

Do not make the mistake of thinking that organised religion is necessarily anti-sex – and this is no mere jibe at the Reverend Jimmy Swaggart. Based on biblical teaching, controlled sex, modelled on the family unit, marriage, self-containment and the goal of procreation is encouraged by many in the field of divinity. And you would be surprised at what you can read in modern religion-based sex manuals – 'the Joy of Christian Sex' being the nickname for the genre. (Porn-again Christianity!)

If God's got something better than sex to offer, he's certainly keeping it to himself.

Sting

RELIGIOUS VALUES

To be carnally minded is death.

Romans 8, 6

The Church has long upheld the virtues of chastity, fidelity and celibacy. Tertullian, Clement of Alexandria, Cyprian and Jerome maintained that an orderly sex life was inferior to no sex life at all. Their example inspired not only monks and nuns through the ages but a wider religious teaching. For those choosing a sanctified path of abstinence or fidelity, there is plenty of heavyweight theological, spiritual, and moral backing.

I do not believe there is total sexual satisfaction outside Jesus Christ.

Dr Billy Graham

Religious Values

Just as the husband has shown an effort of sacrifice and love in gaining complete ejaculatory control, so the wife can also contribute to the relationship by attaining full control and strength in the muscles which surround the lower third of her vagina in order to experience a much more intense sexual stimulation.

Gaye Wheat, Intended for Pleasure:
Sex Technique and Fulfilment
in a Christian Marriage

Only when the Christian Church can say 'thank God for sex' can it begin to respond in any authentic manner to the challenge of the sexual revolution.

Dr David R. Mace,
The Christian Response to the
Sexual Revolution

You will find a unique joy in using all the skill you possess to bring pleasure to your marriage partner. In fact, every physical union should be an exciting contest to see which partner can outplease the other. The husband should be the world's greatest authority on how to please his wife. And the wife should be able to say as joyously as the bride in Song of Solomon: 'I am my beloved's, and his desire is toward me' (7:10).

Ed Wheat, Sex Technique, *etc*

Of all the lusts and desires, there is none so powerful as sexual inclination.

*Buddha, third of Buddhist
precepts on self-control*

We seem to forget that there are other experiences as well as sex that offer great pleasure and fulfilment. Meditation brings a feeling of ecstasy. And this emotion appears to be more possible to people who don't have sexual experience. I've spent time with nuns who were like that. So open and full of joy, so generous of spirit. There was none of that 'shrivelled ovary' syndrome.

Nuns, monks, mystics . . . they've all transmuted their sexual energy onto a higher plane.

Leslie Kenton,
British author and beauty editor

Male and female bodies will be the same after the Resurrection when they enter paradise. However, the need, or desire, for sexual expression will be quenched.

Pope John Paul II

Modesty is the guardian of purity . . . knowledge of evil does not keep people from evil . . . our predecessors got along without all the sex instruction that is now ruining so many under the pretext of educating them. The purest and healthiest nations of the world have been those least acquainted with sex knowledge.

Father Scott in Roman Catholic
pamphlet, Marriage Problems

'Tis the Devil inspires this evanescent ardour, in order to divert the parties from prayer.

Martin Luther

Religious Values

Your wives are your tillage; go in therefore into your tillage in what manner soever ye will.

Mohammed

The Church has been guilty of preserving and preaching a point of view . . . which is not only un-Biblical but also anti-Biblical.

William Graham Cole,
Sex in Christianity and Psychology

I get very sexually excited on stage. It's not just an act . . . up there on stage it's like making love to nine thousand people at once. I feel so very close to God when I'm that aroused. Never closer. Sexual passion and the Good Lord are as high as you can possibly get.

Prince

Wife to priest: 'Before sexual intercourse, my husband and I always say the same familiar prayer.'
Priest: 'What prayer?'
Wife: 'For what we are about to receive, may the Lord make us truly thankful . . .'

Quoted by Dr David R. Mace,
The Christian Response to the
Sexual Revolution

I used to take my Bible with me to orgies . . . everybody likes to go to orgies.

Little Richard

He who too ardently loves his wife is an adulterer.

St Jerome

BEWARE OF BRIEF DELIGHT AND LASTING
SHAME

'Wayside Pulpit' poster

Dancing is full of sexual undertones and the different sexes have to touch each other. No one who fears God would take part in this activity.

Angus Smith,
Rector of Lewis, Hebrides

Prenuptial fornication is supposed to be common in some rural areas. I have had experience of such cases in my own parish, but I have never known a case where a couple alleged they were doing right, or that love was the motive of their act. Usually they confess that they are ashamed.

Reverend A. R. Shillinglaw,
Church of Scotland representative
at the British Council of Churches

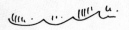

"I'M SORRY LOVE
VIRGIN'S ONLY."

Life-long virginity is the ideal sexual ethic for Christians. For Christians, an orderly sex life is inferior to no sex life at all.

Terry Loughdon, Rector of Nitan
and Chalc, Isle of Wight

SOME SAY YES

Sex is enjoyed by even the highest in the land. Take, for example, the rather splendid case of the knickers in the Minister's out-tray.

The disclosure in April, 1987 that Mrs Jan Brown, wife of Tourism Minister John Brown, had seduced her husband in the corridors of power and settled for a steamy sex-session on his office desk had even Australians perspiring with envy. Yes, Minister.

Mother of five Mrs Brown told a TV audience that she had mounted her ministerial offensive when she found herself, as the wife back home, taking a back seat to more pressing matters of State. 'Suddenly it was the Minister is busy, the Minister hasn't time to see you, the Minister will ring back.'

'So I seduced him on his desk the first day he was in his new office as a Minister. I suppose it was a bit of vindictiveness that I left the undies in the out-tray.' (Private Secretary: 'What action do you require on these, Minister?')

Said Mrs Brown, 44: 'I did it all to show them it was a new order.' Premier Bob Hawke was not so impressed, however, saying he didn't want a repeat performance. *No*, minister.

Other politicians have enjoyed a headline or two in matters sexual, of course. US Congressman John Jenrette even 'made it' with his wife on the steps of the Capitol Building.

Perhaps the member of parliament most closely identified with sex, however, was Italian MP Ilona

OTHERS SAY NO

A revealing insight into changing sexual mores came in a court case in London at the end of April, 1988, when two lovelorn upper-middle-class teenagers were divorced – on the grounds that the schoolboy husband had refused to make love to his wife.

The case of the virgin gymslip bride and her unwilling sixth-form spouse brought much comment in the popular press, not merely of the nudge-nudge, wink-wink variety.

The 'Sloane Ranger' schoolgirl – deputy head girl at her school, and just 19 – and her 19-year-old intended had apparently slipped out of lessons to marry in a registry office ceremony nine months before the hearing. To celebrate, they 'nipped out for a quick drink' but within half an hour had returned to their respective schools in Worcestershire where they were boarders. They never told their parents.

The husband's ardour subsequently cooled, however, despite constant phone calls from the girl. Judge Monier Williams said that the young bride thought it was the intention that they should get a flat and jobs and build a life together. She kept in constant communication with her spouse, but he apparently did not wish to visit her. That came as 'something of a shock' to her.

The judge added that the girl's mother arranged a holiday in Spain and he was invited. But he refused to go, and after her daughter returned from holiday, the sad truth 'came tumbling out'. The young husband

Some Say Yes

'Cuddles' Staller, in her previous life the country's most notorious porn star and proud owner of 'the best-known boobs in Italy'.

In a long statement of policy to British interviewer John Smith in March, 1988, she told how 'I get very nervous if I don't make love every day. It relaxes me,' and 'I know all the positions in the Kama Sutra. And I've tried most of them.'

It was the MP's fervent wish to make a trip to London to see Mrs Thatcher ('to talk about Parliament and sex'), she said, and no doubt some British members would be upstanding in support of that. She told Mr Smith: 'I never made love to an Englishman, but I would like to.'

There is a 'positive link' between brainpower and libido, the genius's organisation MENSA reported in May, 1988. After surveying the club's eighteen thousand members in New York, the intellectual elitists' spokesman said: 'The results show there is a definite relationship between intelligence and sexuality. Better educated appears to mean better between the sheets. Mastermind types are definitely masters in the bedroom.' The *Daily Star* sought to confirm these findings and pronounced disc jockey Tony Blackburn living proof of the research. He said: 'It must be true. I love sex, and I'm the brainiest person I know.'

According to the *Guardian*'s correspondent in Moscow, Martin Walker, sex may have been officially regarded in the Soviet Union until recently as bourgeois Western decadence, but Russians tend to vote with their feet (or at least with other anatomical extremities).

told her he had made a mistake in marrying her.

Said Judge Williams: 'It is a very sad story. It is a shocking way for the girl to start her life after leaving school.'

Granting her a divorce on the grounds of nullity, he said he had 'no hesitation' in saying that her husband had 'wilfully refused to consummate' the match and that the couple had never had intercourse.

No, this is not a fairy tale. Did you know that chilly winter nights are a turn-off for women? Medical experts in December, 1987 even invented a name for the affliction: SAD (seasonal affective disorders). The British Medical Journal reported that some women behave like squirrels when there is an 'r' in the month and go into 'sexual hibernation' during long winter nights. Victims of SAD, said the report, suffered depression often lasting until the spring.

It took many years for them to catch up with the decadent West but in May, 1976, the Soviet Union finally admitted to the existence of . . . sex. The acknowledgement of that to which comrades had certainly some knowledge and experience, if not with official party blessing, came in the form of an entry in the

Some Say Yes

'From my own strolls through parks and country-side,' he wrote in February 1988, 'I can confirm that the Russians are among the world's most enthusiastic practitioners of the splendid art of love-making in the open air. Indeed, in the long grass of Izmailovo Park last summer, a friend of mine was flying a kite and broke his leg when he tripped over one enraptured couple.'

Part of the problem lies in the fact that only a minority in the Soviet Union owns a car. For those who do, the outside temperature is usually enough to freeze the door locks if not the libido. Students and young workers all live in dormitories. Couples cannot check into hotels without papers establishing them as married. The adventurous, muses Mr Walker, might try two tickets on the overnight sleeper from Moscow to Leningrad, though the cost would be 60 roubles – a week's wages.

Consequently, among his Soviet friends, only one in four had not at some time made love in public, or with a thin curtain around to shield them from others in the same room. This must mean silent love-making, he remarked to a friend. 'Who needs to speak when it is all in the eyes,' was the reply.

There is also virtually no Aids in the Soviet Union, so if you can stand the cold, and don't mind the risk of KGB voyeurs, it remains one of the best venues in the world for 'safe sex'.

Quite apart from those 60-rouble bone-shakers in the Soviet Union, the gentle rhythms of a train journey have long led to what we might dub squeals on wheels. In August, 1984, regulars on the 8.52 from London Waterloo to Guildford were treated to such a

Great Soviet Encyclopaedia. There was acknowledgement, too, of Western influence. While the Soviet version was, appropriately enough, a four-letter word in the Cyrillic alphabet CEKC, its pronunciation was, well, the same as in English.

That didn't stop an embarrassing moment in a live TV link-up between audiences in Seattle and Leningrad, however. When an American asked 'What is the attitude to sex in the Soviet Union?' an angry Russian leapt for the microphone and protested: 'What sex? We do not have sex over here.'

By 1988, Glasnost was beginning to change the social map of the Soviet Union, but as the *Daily Telegraph*'s Moscow correspondent, Xan Smiley reported, there remained concern at the hitherto unperestroika'd area of sex education.

Mr Smiley reported that the top Soviet sexologist, the splendidly named Professor I. Kon, had at last managed to publish the first study of sexual behaviour in the USSR, a mere ten years after it was written. But with the joy came the lament that the poor Soviet people still had no sex manual to learn from. 'As far as publishing goes,' said Professor Kon, 'we have been a sexless society.'

Wrote the Soviet sexpert: 'Even today the delicate subject of sexual relations is usually treated with what Engels called "false petit bourgeois modesty". Studies have shown that our boys and girls are woefully ignorant of the anatomy and physiology of sex, not to mention childbirth and child care.'

M'learned judges have long set their stall as innocents in an increasingly sex-dominated society, and 60-year-old Mr Justice Cantley was a typical example when he pronounced in the case of sex and the single man.

display of passionate improvisation that they ended the journey clapping and cheering the two participants.

The journey had begun quietly enough, with several City types busily burying noses in the financial pages. But then the action started and stiff English upper lips began to tremble.

A giggling teenage girl first began to do an impromptu striptease, divesting herself of a tight black leather skirt, followed by a revealing red blouse. She then sank into the arms of a young male companion, pausing briefly to shout before becoming submerged in a deep embrace: 'It's his birthday and this is his present.'

Sadly for the by now captivated business types, the train lurched to a halt at Surbiton, seventeen minutes out of Waterloo, and the giggling girl and her grinning male companion raced off to give up their tickets (or that's what the businessmen benevolently assumed).

A British Rail spokesman said: 'They didn't have much time, did they?'

Still on the railway theme, the famed Orient Express tried to move off from the station at Innsbruck in Austria in September 1984 . . . and nothing happened. The train simply would not budge. Engineers were summoned to examine the locomotive. They found nothing wrong.

Thirty minutes later, in one of the compartments, railway officials found a girl and her boyfriend making love. They were so 'wrapped up in each other' they had failed to notice the girl's foot tangled round the communication cord, thus applying the emergency brake.

The train finally moved off – arriving at its destination some seventy minutes late. ('We regret to announce . . .')

The judge was hearing a High Court case in the 1970s involving a 25-year-old man who was suing for damages over an accident involving a bulldozer. He was told the man's sex life had been affected.

Mr Justice Cantley asked: 'Is he married?'

Mr Kenneth Jones, QC, said: 'No, m'lud.'

'Well,' said the judge. 'I can't see how it affects his sex life.'

Finally, while on the subject of blissful ignorance, we should mention the case of the Taiwan mother of six who was found sobbing hysterically in a Formosa street in March, 1983. Asked what was her predicament, she replied: 'I won't have any more children. A neighbour has just told me what causes them.'

THE MOST FUN I'VE
HAD WITHOUT
LAUGHING . . .

How tall are you, son?
Six feet five and a half inches.
Let's forget about the six feet and talk about the five
and a half inches.

Mae West

Whether or not you believed that it can never replace
the quick grope, the bicycle ride (or the cold shower!)
sex has long been an essential ingredient of humour.
Don't take our word for it. Ask Woody (*Everything You
Always Wanted to Know About Sex, But Were Afraid to
Ask*) Allen . . .

Is sex dirty? Only if it's done right.

Everything You Always
Wanted to Know, Etc

Sex is like having dinner: Sometimes you joke about
the dishes, sometimes you take the meal seriously.

Evening Standard
interview, August 1965

ALL RIGHT, LEAVE IT OUT . . .

Continental people have sex lives; the English have hot water bottles.

George Mikes, How to Be An Alien

Chastity, usually enforced by some malady such as 'brewer's droop' or other ailments, requiring a visit to the doctor's surgery, has long since provided comedians with ammunition for their humour. Then there are the impotence-joke specialists. Like into-the-eighties-in-more-ways-than-one George Burns.

I like going out with young girls. I dance very close – it keeps an old man warm. Listen, when a girl goes out with me, all she has to do is light up my cigar.

Daily Express, *March 1982*

Did I tell you the time I was dropping the great Sophie Tucker home after a party? She was in her sixties and it was way past her bedtime. I parked the car and I said: 'Sophie, I'm out of gas, let's neck.'

'George,' she said, 'We're both out of gas, take me home.'

Sunday Express, *June 1976*

The Most Fun I've Had Without Laughing

I'm a latent heterosexual.
> Daily Express, *January 1976*

In the after-life, I'd like to come back as Warren Beatty's fingertips.
> Woman's Own, *October 1983*

Warren Beatty always insists on buying his date dinner . . . because the rest of the date is on her.
> *quoted in* Daily Express, *1987*

Some more pro-sex humour:

I'm tired. Send one of them home.
> *Mae West, on being told ten men*
> *were waiting to meet her at her apartment*

How many husbands have I had? You mean, apart from my own?
> *Zsa Zsa Gabor*

I go to the theatre to be entertained . . . I don't want to see plays about rape, sodomy and drug addiction. I can get all that at home.
> *Peter Cook*

Dear Marje, If a girl has intercourse and then has nothing more to do with boys for a year, can she become a virgin again?
> *Letter from 'Hopeful' in* Daily Mirror,
> *recalled by 'This England' column,*
> New Statesman

All Right, Leave It Out

Here's a letter:

Dear George, I'm getting along in years and I'm having a problem with my sex life. A friend of mine who's two years older than I am says he has sex three times a week.

So I wrote back and said: 'If he can say it, you can say it.'

How to Live to be 100 – Or More

Some more anti-sex humour:

My father told me all about the birds and the bees. The liar – I went steady with a woodpecker until I was 21.

Bob Hope

I didn't know how babies were made until I was pregnant with my fourth child.

Loretta Lynn

Of course, sending flowers can please. But it can also get you into trouble. Especially if her husband is at home when they are delivered and he has to sign the receipt.

Jack Nicholson
(yes, it happened to him)

The Most Fun I've Had Without Laughing

I am suing Frank Sinatra for support for the four years I
would have lived with him had he asked me.

Joan Rivers

Kissed a boy for the first time today. Very disappointed. It's nothing compared with oral sex.

Joan Rivers,
Heidi's Fourth Grade Diary

What do you give the man who's had everyone?

Alana Stewart on ex-husband Rod

'Which do you think is more important, sex or wine?' asked a rather brash young feminist of a much-travelled wine buff.

The expert thought about it for a moment, then said cautiously: 'Claret or Burgundy?'

Overheard by columnist Colin
Reid at a party

I hate hunks and pin-ups. Just look at Sylvester Stallone. Going to bed with him would be like making love to a coffee table.

Ruby Wax, comedienne

It's been so long since I made love I can't even remember who gets tied up.

Joan Rivers

COME 'SWING' WITH ME

Fifty years ago in films, the boy got the girl. Today it's anybody – her mother, father, brother, or cocker spaniel.

Bob Hope, 1981

It is too easy to start an orgy circle.

News of the World, *1976*

Variety may not always be the spice of life, but when it comes to sexual matters, even the most fundamental of Bible-punchers would accede to there being a certain diversity of taste around. But how much of this is now under threat in these days of Aids?

It is not our intention to do anything but hint at practices such as wife-swapping, ('part of the British way of life' Dr Martin Cole); starting one's own Janet Reger collection from the neighbour's washing line; Freeman, Hardy and Willis worship, etc. But, well, the world of the 'swinger', however diminishing, does provide plenty to laugh at.

LET'S KEEP IT CLEAN . . .

If one of my sons came home and said he was living with a girl, I'd never speak to him again.

Bing Crosby, 1977

Mummy, could you keep your knickers on just once? I'm getting hell from the chaps at school.

Arthur, 9, to his mother, film
siren Sylvia Kristel, quoted in the
Daily Express, *1984*

For every 'swinger', it must be agreed, there are many more more traditional thinkers who believe in monogamy ('I believe in it – sequentially, of course' Joan Collins); many who are convinced sexuality can be full of cleanliness as well as godliness; and other innocents who would think whipping is a dessert topping, bondage something to do with customs warehouses, pederasty a form of chiropody, and a transvestite some sort of character out of a Dracula horror film.

Their numbers are inevitably increasing in the new age of fidelity.

Come Swing With Me

No Sensuous Couple can claim to have a full repertoire of sex techniques unless they make full use of the bath and the shower.

> 'Doctor "C"',
> The Sensuous Couple

Motorcycle: Increasingly popular sexual venue, which combines the symbolism of the horse with leather gear, danger, and acceleration. Has serious safety drawbacks . . .

> *Dr Alex Comfort*, The Joy of Sex

Sally and Jane Lambert, in Angela Pearson's *The Whipping Club*, illustrate the posture most effectively. They lie on a divan with their heads at opposite ends. Each has her big toe thrust inside the vulva of the other and their bodies agitated vigorously against the toes. This is the only method of intercourse which will allow a man to enjoy sexual satisfaction and drink whisky, smoke a cigar and read a book at the same time.

> *John Atkins*, Sex in Literature

I have a great interest in rolling on PVC sheets, smothered in olive oil, with 16-year-old skinny broilers.

> *Rat Scabies, The Damned*

" OH DARLING ... YOU ARE SO SENSUOUS "

Sex, sex, sex, too much sex. Everywhere in the stores, sex, sex, sex, too much sex.

> *Peter Kozlov, exchange Soviet*
> *student at Georgetown*
> *University, Washington, 1965*

My code is chastity before marriage and fidelity within it.

> *Mary Whitehouse, 1981*

Dr Comfort's ideal pair would appear to be a couple of Habitat acrobats with more money than sensuality who dream of a boudoir rigged as a 'sexual gymnasium' (swings and trapezes optional extras) with floor mattresses as well as beds; ceiling mirrors; posts for 'bondage scenes'; low-level cupboards for lubricants, contraceptives, vibrators, Polaroid cameras, tape recorders and pornography; wardrobes for costumes, boots and masks. If you tot up the bill, it would be cheaper to keep a string of polo ponies.

> *Alan Brien,* Sunday Times,
> *reviewing* The Joy of Sex, *1974*

I don't sleep with other women and I don't miss making love. I can go for at least a month and not notice it. I use up a lot of sexual energy in my performances and, after a concert, I'm so exhausted that I just want to go back to the hotel and sleep.

> *Richard Clayderman, pianist, on*
> *touring,* Titbits, *1984*

Come Swing With Me

'Can you please fix it for me to meet the girls on page 39 of the Mothercare catalogue. I would like them to chase me through the woods and tie me to a tree.'

Letter from 'six year old' to Jimmy Savile of BBC's Jim'll Fix It

When I glimpse the backs of women's knees I seem to hear the first movement of Beethoven's *Pastoral Symphony*.

Article in Daily Mail, *quoted by 'This England' column,* New Statesman

'My husband likes to wear my bra when he's making love to me. Is this abnormal?'

Letter to Dr David Delvin, Titbits, *1983*

Smoke everything you can, including your pubic hair.

Yoko Ono, 1971

'Take my horse to his own bed.'

Mind-boggling deviant imperial command from the film Caligula *(what else)*

" FOR HEAVEN'S SAKE DARLING, IT'S FASHIONAB

Of course, Salvador Dali seduced many ladies, particularly American heiresses; but these seductions usually entailed stripping them naked in his apartment, frying a couple of eggs, putting them on the women's shoulders, and, without a word, showing them the door.

Film director Luis Buñuel quoted in the Daily Mirror

I have always been cautious when it comes to who I sleep with – I wouldn't even consider going to bed with anyone and everyone. You just have to be careful. Aids isn't the only sexual disease going anyway.

Ben Volpierre of Curiosity Killed the Cat, Ms *magazine, 1987*

You can't fill the bed with groupies. I don't want to be a swinger.

John Lennon, Rolling Stone

I began kissing him passionately. I wanted him – I was ready to submit entirely to him. He returned my passion. Then, abruptly, he stopped.

'Wait a minute, Baby,' he said. 'This can get out of hand.'

Priscilla Presley on the frustrations of dating Elvis

SO GAY'S OK?

There is probably no sensible heterosexual alive who is not preoccupied with his or her latent homosexuality.
Norman Mailer, Advertisement
for Myself

No anthology about sex could possibly be complete without a look at homosexuality, particularly in view of Dr Kinsey's discovery that thirty-eight per cent of US males in 1949 had had homosexual experiences of some kind. 'Gays' are naturally also at the forefront of the Aids debate. Many who are artistically inclined have admitted to Kinsey-type experiences. Lord Byron joked to his tutor that he wished to contribute a chapter to a book by Hobhouse called *Sodomy Simplified, or Pederasty Proved to be Praiseworthy*. When asked whether *his* first experience had been hetero- or homosexual, US writer Gore Vidal replied: 'I was too polite to ask.'

KEEP IT STRAIGHT

I have nothing against giving gays rights. I just don't like them having sex together.

Howard Stern, WNBC dee-jay

Homosexuality is an issue which brings out strong passions, on either side of the closet. And this has nothing to do with the Aids epidemic – you can go right back to the Bible and Leviticus: 'If a man lie with mankind as he lieth with a woman, both of them shall have committed an abomination: they shall surely be put to death.' In recent years, organisations like the Moral Majority in the US have taken up the cudgels for the 'queer-bashers', demanding that homosexual behaviour 'should be coupled with murder and other sins', and talking of capital punishment.

Politicians have found themselves increasingly pressed to woo the gay vote. They do not always obey gracefully. Asked at a meeting what he would do for the civil rights of twenty million homosexuals in the US, Congressman Wilbur Mills said: 'If there are twenty million of them, I'm getting out of here!' While one-time White House hopeful Ed Muskie opined: 'Goddam it, if I've got to be nice to a bunch of sodomites, then f——it.'

So Gay's OK?

Bisexuality – it immediately doubles your chances of a date on a Saturday night.

Woody Allen

Artistic aptitude of one kind or another, and a love of music, are found among a large proportion of educated inverts, in my experience as much as sixty per cent.

Havelock Ellis, pioneer sexologist

God goes out in life to his children, whether they are heterosexual or homosexual, or whether they are a bit of both as many are.

Dr Coggan, Archbishop of Canterbury, 1979

I'd like to return to the sexual sophistication of the better parts of ancient society where you'd say 'I'm in love' and be asked 'is it a boy or a girl'.

Stephen Coote, editor of The Penguin Book of Homosexual Verse

There are no victims, only heroes. They are suffering for all of us.

Contributor to Channel 4's Right to Reply, *1988, objecting to the label 'Aids victims' on television news*

" WELL To BE HONE
WHAT

92

RE NOT QUITE
PECTED "

Keep It Straight

If homosexuality were the normal way, God would
have made Adam and Bruce.

Anita Bryant, US anti-gay
campaigner

Fairies: nature's attempt to get rid of soft boys by
sterilising them.

F. Scott Fitzgerald, The Crack Up

Let it be understood that homosexual indulgence is a
shameful vice and a grievous sin from which deliver-
ance is to be sought by every means.

Dr Fisher, Archbishop of
Canterbury, 1954

This sort of thing may be tolerated by the French, but
we are British, thank God.

Viscount Montgomery, 1965

. . . Swirling round in a cesspit of their own making.

Greater Manchester Chief
Constable James Anderton on
homosexuals, 1987

So Gay's OK?

American gay men are now visible, accepted – as much as a quarter of San Francisco's adult population is said to be homosexual. No longer are they only hairdressers and ballet dancers; the man sporting a tinsel tut in Christopher Street could be a successful broker on Wall Street – or even a New York cop. Edward Kennedy and Hollywood court them. Affluent and politically organised, they are America's new, fashionable minority. People want them as neighbours – 'they take such good care of the place.'

Harriet Sergeant, Sunday
Telegraph, *1982*

I believe the nearest I have come to perfect love was with a young coal-miner when I was about 16.

D. H. Lawrence

We must recognise the fact that love, whether it be between man and woman or man and man, can achieve a pure and glorious relationship providing it is expressed with restraint and discipline. And that is true of all sexual relationships.

*Dr Mervyn Stockwood, Bishop of
Southwark, 1979*

We are all fallen beings and homosexuals are no more fallen than you or me.

*Dr David Stacey, chairman of
Methodist Church working party
on sexuality, 1979*

Tchaikovsky thought of committing suicide for fear of being discovered as a homosexual, but today, if you are a composer and *not* homosexual you might as well put a bullet through your head.

Sergei Diaghilev, quoted by Frank
S. Pepper in Twentieth Century
Quotations

Homosexuality is a sickness, just as are baby-rape or wanting to become head of General Motors.

Eldridge Cleaver

My own feeling is that logically homosexuality isn't natural, it isn't the norm. I'm not saying that people of the same sex can't have perfectly good relationships, but I don't see how the Church can actually embrace it, or imply that homosexuality is 'all right'.

Cliff Richard

Everything is controlled by the sods. The country is riddled with homosexuals who are teaching the world how to behave – a spectacle of revolting hypocrisy.

Sir Thomas Beecham, quoted by
Charles Reed, Beecham: An
Independent Biography

So Gay's OK?

If one can speak of a 'normal' state, it is bisexuality. I am quite sure that if you could bring up a child without any gender conditioning, that child would be bisexual.

Dr Charlotte Wolff, Fellow of the British Psychological Society

As a lifestyle choice, lesbianism is looking better than it ever has. No pregnancies, contraception complications, AIDS or husbands to hold one down; a life of potentially permanent teenage kicks and camaraderie.

Julie Burchill, the Mail on Sunday *(an iconoclast, it must be said, rather than an enthusiast)*

When it comes to love, woman is the perfect instrument. From head to toes she is made solely, miraculously for love. *She alone* knows how to love; *she alone* knows how to be loved. Therefore, if a loving couple is made up of two women it is perfect. If it has only one it is only half perfect. If it has none it is simply idiotic.

from Piere Louÿs, Aphrodite

Keep It Straight

It doesn't seem much more fun for a woman to be bedded by a woman as an affirmation of feminism than wedded by a man to provide heirs for his property.

Brigid Brophy, Sunday Times

Of course lesbians must have legal marriages. The children have to be considered.

Dorothy Parker

Two girls in a bed, that's awful. A man and a girl is fine, but two members of the same sex – ugh! That's disgusting.

Hugh Hefner

A DOCTOR WRITES: EIGHT REASONS WHY SEX IS GOOD FOR YOU

The medical profession, as earlier chapters of this book testify, has long been at the forefront of discovery about human sexuality. And sexual activity, according to pioneers in the field, can benefit you in ways only Hollywood producers have in the past had time to dream about. It is not true that regular indulgence can cure beri-beri, colour blindness, Portnoy's complaint, toe-curl – some ailments you could only find in a Swedish medical directory or a Turkish phone book!

Sex is good for you, according to the medics, and here are some of the reasons why.

1. *IT KEEPS YOU SLIM, IT KEEPS YOU FIT*

According to Dr Abraham Friedman, who wrote a book called *How Sex Can Keep You Slim* ('Reach for your mate instead of your plate'), approximately 200 calories are burned during 'the act', resulting in a 900 calorie bonus if an overweight person forgoes his or her nightly Horlicks and chocolate biscuit and dives enthusiastically beneath the blankets instead.

French courtesan Madame Dubarry was beautifully thin when she had lovers, he argued, but in line with the unhappy rejected all over the world, piled on the pounds when there was no one there to whom she could offer her considerable charms. 'Make love, not fat,' advised the good doctor.

A DOCTOR WRITES:
EIGHT REASONS WHY
SEX IS BAD FOR YOU

Not that we are accusing them of being a morbid profession, but doctors through the ages have linked every form of physical activity, especially those involving pleasure, with some incurable disease. Just so with sex, and keeping a clean bill of health remains the prime non-spiritual justification for celibacy. Is it not true that this base animal instinct can give you acne, blindness, whooping cough, gout, housemaid's knee, tennis elbow, Achilles heel, and a succession of allergies reading like the menu in a French Grand Hotel?

Sex is bad for you, according to the experts, because . . .

1. *IT CAN'T KEEP YOU SLIM, IT CAN'T KEEP YOU FIT*

According to top sports physician Dr Gabe Mirkin of the University of Maryland, sex is a waste of time from the physical fitness point of view, whatever its apologists and their calorie calculations say. 'During an hour of lively sex, someone can only expect to lose 250 calories.' And – wait for it – 'Most people can't manage that.'

The pulse rate only quickens, according to Dr Mirkin, during the love act because of hormones released from adrenal glands. Making love is only the equivalent of walking up two flights of stairs at a moderate

Reasons Why Sex Is Good For You

British physicians Stephen Lock and Anthony Smith also reported in the British Medical Journal that regular sex is a major boost to getting in trim. One average sex session is equivalent to twenty press-ups for keeping heart disease at bay, they calculated.

2. IT'S THE PERFECT CURE FOR HEADACHES

Sex is more effective than analgesics for curing headaches, according to British medic Dr John Smith. Announcing the results of a Gallup survey in the *Daily Mail* in October, 1987, Dr Smith reported that a good 'kiss and a cuddle' relaxes muscles in the neck and shoulders that trigger troublesome headaches.

'Most headaches arise from muscle tension and the best way to relieve that is to be stroked by someone who loves you,' he advised.

3. IT CAN HELP FIGHT CORONARIES

According to Professor Harry Brodyr of Calgary University, Canada: 'Sex is good for the heart.'

It is also 'one of nature's finest tonics,' according to Dr Thomas P. Hackett, chief of psychiatry at the Massachusetts Hospital, Boston. In 1982, Dr Hackett

pace. His view – you'd be better off just jogging twice round the block.

2. *IT CAN GIVE YOU ANGINA*

Sex is one of the major causes of sudden attacks of angina, particularly 'if painful or causing anxiety', according to Dr Harley Williams, director general of the Chest and Heart Association and author of a definitive pamphlet in 1976, *Learning to Live With Angina*.

Bed, rather than sex, is important too, and Dr Williams warned that sudden moves to slip beneath chilly sheets can be equally blamed for causing attacks. So no sudden frenzied bursts of passion, please. If you do want to say, 'take me, take me now' etc. to your partner, make sure you have lined up a hot water bottle, bed warmer, or turned the electric blanket on first.

(The authors suggest the IBA and film censors might take the lead in this important matter. Henceforth, all seduction scenes should include this compulsory exchange:

'You *are* going to take precautions?'

'Yes (holds up synthetic rubber apparatus to camera), I've got a full pint-and-a-half water bottle.')

3. *IT CAN CAUSE CORONARIES*

Sexual activity is, of course, physically jerksome. It is estimated that without sexual intercourse or football, half the orthopaedic specialists in the US would be redundant overnight. Another researcher estimated that the g forces engendered in an hour's sexual

said that sex was a positive aid to recovery for heart attack victims. 'People who return to a sexual life almost invariably have a better prognosis in terms of returning to work . . . and to socialising.' It is 'a damaging myth', he said, 'that once you have a coronary you're over the hill and there's no sense in even talking about sex because you can't have it anymore.'

His view echoes that of Dr Terry Davison, a cardiologist at the Long Island Jewish Hillside Medical Centre, who in 1971 pronounced sex 'one of the best forms of exercise for heart patients'.

4. IT'S THE PERFECT CURE FOR INSOMNIA
A report in the July 1987 edition of *Drugs and Therapeutics Bulletin* recommended 'non-drugs strategies' for people suffering anxiety or sleeplessness. The three suggested alternatives were a dull book, a relaxing bath . . . or sexual intercourse.

Commenting on the findings, Dr Andrew Her-

activity by a couple under the age of 35 was roughly equivalent to the stress of a 90 mph gale on the Golden Gate Bridge, San Francisco, or the forces on a pilot in a F-14 Tomcat during a total of eight weeks of training. But he was joking and no one believed him.

What is universal truth is that for the married, middle-aged boss, a willing young girlfriend can prove a real life 'fatal attraction'. An American study in 1977 showed that of 114 men who died while making love, 90 were prosperous mid-life menopausals over-doing it with a young mistress.

Professor Bernhard Krauland who mounted the study for West Berlin University said: 'Sex outside the marriage is dangerous for the heart because it can prove too exciting.'

Another survey in 1983 by New York University psychologists, Donald Fraser and Janet Walsh, found that more married executives died from heart attacks brought on by the strain of having an affair with another member of staff than from the stress of every-day work.

And the problem of over-enthusiastic over-exertion by the unfit businessman on the first day of his vacation prompted another doctor, West German professor Max Halhuber, to urge in 1972: 'Don't overdo the sex at the start of your holiday. It can kill. Take sex on an instalment plan. Take it easy at first.'

4. IT CAN CAUSE ARTHRITIS

Up to five hundred painful arthritis cases a year in Great Britain, particularly among the young, are the results of sexual intercourse, you may be surprised to know. No, it is not joints a-creaking from too much physical contortion, but the result of a sexually trans-mitted bacteria, *chlamydia trachomatis*, which finds its

scheimer, clinical pharmacologist at Charing Cross Hospital, London, said: 'Sex is an enjoyable experience in itself and produces one of the most pleasant forms of sleep.'

5. IT CAN HELP YOUR CAREER AT THE OFFICE

In a book entitled *Stress Without Distress*, Dr Hans Selye, director of the Institute of Medicine and Surgery at Montreal University, was to promote this unsophisticated but resonant slogan for the 1970s: 'Nothing succeeds like sexcess.'

'You can't beat love,' purred the doctor. 'The longer you keep active sexually, the better your prospects of staying in front at work.'

It may have given way later to the jogging craze, of course, but he was quick to point out: 'To keep fit we must exercise our bodies and our minds.' Work life could not succeed without sex life, he opined.

And if sex at the office was out? Then change your job, said the doctor. 'Try to find playful professions,' he advised.

In 1984, a psychologist studying work and love in the Common Market (hereafter called 'the sex mountain') found that people worked harder if they were having an affair with someone from the same company.

6. IT MAKES THE BEARD GROW

It was well known in medieval times. Tshao Mu Tzu was one who wrote: 'The after glory of the seminal essence is manifested by the beard.' More recently came the finding of a Cambridge University scientist,

way into the joints. According to Dr John Dixey at Westminster Hospital, London, a rheumatologist who became involved in a £52,000 research project into arthritis and sex in 1987: 'The disease can be very painful, requiring drug treatment for several months. In nine out of ten cases it eventually fades away but it can go on to be a chronic condition.'

5. IT CAN MAKE YOU INFERTILE
Too much of it, anyway. Dr D. R. London, consultant physician at Queen Elizabeth Hospital, Edgbaston, Birmingham, suggested in 1972 that over-indulgence might be a reason why one in ten couples were unable to have a baby, and advised his colleagues always to inquire of sterile couples how many times intercourse had taken place. 'Too frequent intercourse or masturbation can lower the sperm count to subfertile levels,' he advised grimly in the *British Medical Journal.*

6. IT CAN GIVE YOU ULCERS
One of the favourite times for sex is, of course, after a meal. Indulgents might be feeling restful and relaxed . . . but is it good for the digestion?

An emphatic *no* from US doctor Dr Tom de Meester

duly recorded in the magazine *Nature* in 1970. The truth had dawned on the hirsute boffin, he wrote after several weeks isolation on a remote island. When he was due to return home, his whiskers began to sprout. The day before he was reunited with his wife, the growth became quite frenzied.

The latter-day Ben Gunn then embarked on a controlled research project, watching his beard sprout in anticipation of sex sessions he deliberately restricted to weekends only over ten-day periods. His suitably rational explanation was that the secretion of certain hormones, normally androsterone, in expectation of 'the act' could turn a particularly smooth man into a much hairier one.

In 1988 came total confirmation of his thesis with an article in the *Lancet* by four doctors based at Rouen in France. They cited the case of a *woman* – herself a doctor – who grew stubble after each night of passion with her husband. 'SEX ROMP WIFE GROWS A BEARD' – *Daily Star*.

The medics reported 'excessive facial hair growth with a distinctly male pattern' and considered what drugs she was taking. The answer? None, apart from the contraceptive pill. A little French detective work then tracked down the culprit . . . hormone cream which the *husband* was using to try and improve his sexual performance. Somehow, it had reached the parts of his wife his new-found ardour could never have anticipated.

7. IT CAN STOP YOU SNEEZING

Not that sex can cure the common cold . . . but doctors around the world have observed that couples with healthy sex lives are less prone to sneezes and sniffles than those with emotional hang-ups.

at an international conference in Florence in 1984.
'After a good meal,' he told delegates, 'it is better not
to nap, smoke, drink, worry, or worse . . . make love.
All of them can be the cause of bad digestion resulting
in ulcers.'

"STRANGE, THEY'RE STILL NOT WORKING"

7. IT CAN MAKE YOU SNEEZE!

Derby allergy expert Dr Harry Morrow Brown re-
vealed in a book in 1985 that one of his patients had
been turned into a nervous wreck, because every time
he went into the bedroom for a sex session with his

Reasons Why Sex Is Good For You

A study by Dr Malcolm Haydon-Baillie at Worksop, Notts, in 1983 found that patients had cold symptoms eased by coupling. They reported that stuffy, blocked-up feelings disappeared and they could breathe normally, with a clear head, for several hours after sex sessions.

He said: 'Proprietary cold medicines are expensive, while loving is free. And I'm sure it's much better for you.'

8. IT'S INEXPENSIVE

Well, usually. And, as we are mostly considering the medical implications, it is also available off-prescription. Dr Frederick Lishman, medical officer of health for Mere and Tisbury, Wiltshire, backed sex not only as an aid to staying slim but for its financial properties in keeping the pounds down.

'It's cheap,' he said. 'Whatever else you say about love, you can't beat it as a cure for inflation.'

GRAPEFRUIT JUICE
The sexual signals sent out by certain squeezed citrus fruits are quite something, if Italian actor Maurizio Arena is to be believed. In a magazine interview in the 1970s he told how, at the age of 38, he had made love to some 18,000 women (or two a night for 24 years) – 'Only slightly fewer than the population of Tonbridge,' one newspaper pointed out. And the secret of his seductive prowess? Twelve glasses of grapefruit juice a day. His technique, having swallowed said juice was, he said: 'Never go too fast with them. The result? None of them ever say no.' ('Old fruit . . .')

Mr Arena was backed by British psychiatrist Dr Gerald Camber, who said: 'Grapefruit juice is rich in Vitamin C, which builds strong bodies and gives energy. Health, inclination, imagination and time are the ingredients for a great lover.'

Even if you don't believe he really had all those women, you would definitely have to believe him when he said he never had a cold in 24 years.

wife, he suffered violent sneezing fits. The 36-year-old man's problem was brought on by emotional stress, said the doctor. He advised: 'Try to make love where there is as little dust as possible.' Hay fever sufferers who have ever made love in cornfields, haystacks, etc., may already be familiar with the problem.

8. IT CAN BORE YOU TO DEATH

The sex enthusiasts may argue that you cannot have too much of a good thing, but scientific research confirms that you *can* have too much sex.

An American project in 1972 which looked into ways of treating the oversexed found that over-exposure to pornography was a sure route to tedium.

Twenty-three men, aged 21 to 23, took part in the project at the University of North Carolina Medical School. Every day they were deluged with porno-graphic films, novels, and magazines.

According to the British GP's magazine *Pulse*, by the end of the project, the once eager young bucks were completely bored. Two months after the experiment ended, they were still 'turned off completely' from sex.

THE FUTURE . . .

Sex is soulful, it's in our roots. It's where we all came from and it's what we're all about.

Prince

So into the future, joyfully? Despite even the gloomiest prognosis about Aids, sex was far from down and out in 1988. Just before Christmas, Miss Tuppy Owens, founder of the Sex Maniac's Diary, was putting the final touches to her annual Sex Maniac's Ball. ('Come dressed to fulfil your fantasy.') She told *Time Out*: 'There was such a great atmosphere at last year's ball. There was one brilliant spastic guy who won a black rubber sheath that someone had put in the tombola, and he got stripped off and put this dildo on and he just looked so hysterically funny in this wheelchair with an enormous grin on his face . . . I just see it all as a liberating experience.' The same issue of the magazine meanwhile reported 'no let up' in the demand for young male prostitutes ('rent boys') in London's West End. One enthusiastic member of the clan, 'Peter', said the Aids factor had actually increased demand. 'One punter told me he wanted to get in and have a go "before it's too late".'

THE FUTURE . . .

The sexual revolution is not yet dead – it's just that some of the troops are dying.

Masters and Johnson, Crisis:
Sexual Choices in the Age of Aids

So what does the future hold? It is undeniable that sexual mores have undergone a rethink in the second half of the eighties: but the choice remains an individual one. Reflective of his time is TV chat show host, Jonathan Ross: 'I think everyone should fancy lots and lots of different people, but you should only really be bonking one.' Not for him sleeping around. He prefers flirting ('a great game, generally a lot more fun and a lot less disappointing than doing it afterwards'). Or in the words of a single American 26-year-old girl interviewed by Masters and Johnson: 'Let's face it – sex just isn't the most important thing in life. I'm certainly not opposed to sex and I used to enjoy sex, but right now the safest choice for me is no sex at all. No sex, no worries. No sex, no Aids. It's really a very simple equation.'

The Future

If it wasn't for sex, men would kill every woman in the world within 48 hours.

Conversation overheard by
Ms Magazine, *1978*

To get what they want, young women in Hollywood offer the only thing they have, their bodies. I think this is OK now. Women have the right to do as men have always done, use their power for sex.

Angie Dickinson

I love that. I like to pick up a chick, get it together after two or three hours then get up at three o'clock in the morning after about half an hour's sleep. I have so much energy that I'm up, raring to go and write a song. I think it's wonderfully healthy to be an old slag.

Bill Wyman

I think it's better to get the love-making side over fairly speedily and get down to a serious relationship without the desire and rejection situation hanging over you. I'm happy to make love after the first hour.

Michael Winner

If you are going to have sex in the United States today, you are going to have to take the risk of getting herpes.

Dr Kevin Murphy, US researcher into a disease which in 1982 was estimated to affect thirty per cent of the sexually active population

The more sex becomes a non-issue in people's lives, the happier they are.

Shirley MacLaine

Sex today is a matter of life and death. A few years ago it was merely an issue of morality . . . but not any longer. When I was in my late teens, I went through a period of bed-hopping, but I wouldn't do that any more. I look at some guys who are maybe in their late thirties and forties and they are still doing it. Don't they realise they are playing with their lives?

George Michael

I *do* know what the world's coming to and that's a fact. It's coming to complete moral and mental disintegration. We all know that sex orgies, flagellation, homosexuality and procuring have gone on since the beginning of recorded time, but never before has it been so widely and vulgarly and lasciviously publicised.

Noel Coward, Diaries, 1963 (just *after the Profumo affair)*

113

The Future

Everybody I know has a different idea of love. One girl I know said: 'I knew he loved me when he didn't come in my mouth.'

Andy Warhol

Sex is the laughter of genius, it's the bathroom of your mind.

Malcolm McLaren

I CAUGHT MY HUSBAND WEARING A DRESS IN BED WITH MY MUM

Headline in News of the World

All life is a sexual experience.

Holly Johnson

Nowadays it seems to be the girls who do most of the pulling, which is one thing I can't put up with. In fact this age lacks respect and romance. There's not enough real feeling. It's just knickers off and go.

Oliver Tobias

In my experience, teenage sex was always safe sex because it never actually happened.

Craig Brown, Sunday Times

I can't abide promiscuity. Searching for something you never find. Young people are all faithful now. They're very pure.

Toyah Wilcox

Girls scream to sleep with me – but I hate it. I can't tell you how much it turns me off. I know a hell of a lot of pop stars who have as much sex as they can and think what a laugh it is. That's fine for them but, to me, sex is more precious.

Clark Datchler, Johnny Hates Jazz

The Future

My generation were pretty lucky . . . Well, we did everything, which was great, but the new generation can't do anything, go anywhere without a condom. And, in any case, condoms don't always work. They break, they fall off. If I could design one I'd have it made out of thick rubber – Pirelli tyre rubber – and have it designed like a jockstrap, with a sort of hook round the back so it won't come off. They always come off when I'm doing it.

Grace Jones

Isn't it interesting how the sounds are the same for an awful nightmare and great sex?

Rue McClanahan, Blanche
Devereaux in Golden Girls

Tribe sex is the sex of the future.

Dr Alex Comfort

Yes – I haven't had enough sex.

John Betjeman, asked on a BBC2
special if there was anything in
life he regretted

If sex is all wrong and dirty, then I suppose we will have to rethink the human race.

Kenneth Tynan

Sex? I think it is here to stay.

Groucho Marx

116

There is also a sturdy trades unionist and worker inside my head who keeps on grumbling: why do we spend all our time talking about sex when outside in the real world Thatcher and Reagan . . .

Elizabeth Wilson, Guardian

We are now seeking a balance. We realise that revolving-door sex is not the answer to true love and commitment.

Henry Abraham, Boston psychiatrist quoted by Time

When you hit your limit with sex, instead of trying new and different people, new positions, why not look for something else?

Gabrielle Brown, author, The New Celibacy: Why More Men and Women are Abstaining from Sex – and Enjoying It

When you are 76 your thoughts don't often stray to copulation.

Lord Hailsham

I make love to my VCR a lot.

'Jack', homosexual, quoted in Newsweek, *1986*

When all is said and done, more is said than done.

Professor Hans Eysenck

BIBLIOGRAPHY

Aristophanes, *Ecclesiazusae*, William Heinemann, 1924
Atkins, John, *Sex in Literature* (2 vol), Calder and Boyers, 1970
Barrow, Andrew, *The Flesh is Weak*, Hamish Hamilton, 1980
Birmingham, Stephen, *Jacqueline Bouvier Kennedy Onassis*, Victor Gollancz, 1979
Bloomsbury Book of Quotations, Bloomsbury Publishing, 1987
Bresler, Fenton, *The Mystery of Georges Simenon*, William Heinemann, 1983
Brown, Gabrielle, *The New Celibacy: Why More Men and Women are Abstaining From Sex –
    and Enjoying It*, McGraw-Hill, 1980
Brown, Helen Gurley, *Sex and the Single Girl*, Frederick Muller, 1963
Brown, Michele and O'Connor, Ann, *Woman Talk: A Woman's Book of Quotes*, Mac-
    donald, 1984
Brown, Michele and O'Connor, Ann, *Woman Talk II*, Macdonald, 1985
Burgess, Anthony, *Ernest Hemingway and His World*, Thames and Hudson, 1978
Burns, George, *How to Live to 100 – Or More*, Robson Books, 1983
Casanova, Giacomo, *History of My Life* (2 vol), Longmans Green, 1967
Cassell's Book of Humorous Quotations, Cassell, 1969
Cohen, J. M. and M. J. (Ed.), *The Penguin Dictionary of Modern Quotations*, (2nd Ed.),
    Penguin, 1980
Comfort, Dr Alex, *The Joy of Sex*, (Revised Ed.), Mitchell Beazley, 1986
Dalton, David, *The Rolling Stones: The First 20 Years*, Thames and Hudson, 1987
Daly, Mary, *Pure Lust*, The Women's Press, 1984
De Beauvoir, Simone, *The Marquis de Sade*, John Calder, 1963
De Cossart, Michael, *The Food of Love*, Hamish Hamilton, 1978
Delvin, Dr David, *The Book of Love*, NEL, 1974
Doctor 'C', *The Sensuous Couple*, NEL, 1971
Dworkin, Andrea, *Intercourse*, Secker and Warburg, 1987
Ekland, Britt, *True Britt*, Sphere, 1980
Ellis, Havelock, *My Life*, (New Ed.), 1967
Ephron, Nora, *Heartburn*, Pan Books, 1986
Evans, Peter, *Ari: The Life and Times of Aristotle Socrates Onassis*, Jonathan Cape, 1986

Eysenck, H. J. and Wilson, Glenn, *The Psychology of Sex*, J. M. Dent, 1979

Fleming, Karl and Fleming, Anne Taylor, *The First Time*, Simon and Schuster, New York, 1975

Flesch, R., *The Book of Unusual Quotations*, Cassell, 1979

Forrester, Wendy, *Great Grandmother's Weekly: Girl's Own Paper 1880–1901*, Lutterworth, 1980

Friedman, Abraham, *How Sex Can Keep You Slim*, Paul Elek, 1974

Gadney, Reg, *Kennedy*, Macdonald, 1983

Green, Jonathan, *A Dictionary of Contemporary Quotations*, Pan Books, 1982

Green, Jonathan, *Sweet Nothings*, Sphere, 1984

Halliwell, Leslie, *The Filmgoer's Book of Quotes*, Hart-Davis MacGibbon, 1973

Harris, Frank, *My Life and Loves*, W. H. Allen, 1964

Hays, H. R., *The Dangerous Sex*, Methuen, 1966

Himmelfarb, Gertrude, *Marriage and Morals Among the Victorians*, Faber & Faber, 1986

Hite, Shere, *Women and Love: A Cultural Revolution in Progress*, Viking Press, 1988

Hodgkinson, Liz, *Sex Is Not Compulsory*, Columbus, 1986

Hurwood, Bernhardt J., *The Golden Age of Erotica*, Tandem, 1968

Jakubowski, Maxim, *The Wit and Wisdom of Rock and Roll*, George Allen and Unwin, 1983

Johnson, William and Masters, Virginia, *Crisis: Heterosexual Behaviour in the Age of Aids*, Weidenfeld & Nicholson, 1988

Johnson, William and Masters, Virginia, *Human Sexual Inadequacy*, Bantam, 1980

Kassoria, Dr Irene, *Nice Girls Do!*, Granada, 1981

Kelleher, Anne, *Sex Within Reason*, Jonathan Cape, 1987

Leigh, Wendy, *Speaking Frankly: What Makes a Woman G.I.B.*, Muller, 1978

Leigh, Wendy, *What Makes a Man G.I.B.*, Frederick Muller, 1980

Lutyens, Mary, *The Ruskins and the Grays*, John Murray, 1972

Mailer, Norman, *Advertisements for Myself*, Panther, 1970

Mailer, Norman, *The Prisoner of Sex*, Weidenfeld & Nicholson, 1971

Marcus, Stephen, *The Other Victorians*, Weidenfeld & Nicholson, 1964

Meredith, Scott, *G. S. Kaufman and the Algonquin Round Table*, Allen and Unwin, 1974

Metcalf, Fred (Ed.), *The Penguin Book of Modern Humorous Quotations*, Viking Press, 1986

Middles, Mick, *The Smiths*, Omnibus, 1985

Mikes, George, *How to Be An Alien*, André Deutsch, 1984

Morton, Andrew, *The Royal Yacht Britannia*, Orbis, 1981

Munshower, Susan, *Warren Beatty*, W. H. Allen, 1983

Bibliography

Nicholson, Hubert, *Half My Days and Nights*, Autolyons Publications, 1982

Palmer, Myles, *Woody Allen*, Proteus, New York, 1980

Parker, Dorothy, *A Month of Saturdays by 'Constant Reader'*, Viking Press, 1970

Payn, Graham and Morley, Sheridan (Ed.), *The Noel Coward Diaries*, Papermac, 1983

Pepper, Frank S. (Ed.), *Twentieth Century Quotations*, Sphere, 1984

Peter, Laurence J., *Quotations for Our Time*, William Morrow, New York, 1977

Rivers, Joan, *The Life and Times of Heidi Abromowitz*, W. H. Allen, 1984

Roberts, Elizabeth, *A Woman's Place: An Oral History of Working Class Women, 1890–1940*, Blackwell, 1984

Rolling Stone, *The Rolling Stone Interviews*, Arthur Barker, 1981

Rose, Phyllis, *Parallel Lives: Five Victorian Marriages*, Chatto and Windus, 1984

Rousseau, Jean-Jacques, *The Confessions*, Penguin, 1953

Russell, Dora, *The Tamarisk Tree: My Quest for Liberty and Love*, Elell, 1975

Sade, Marquis de, *The 120 Days of Sodom*, Grove Press, 1966

St Augustine, *Confessions*, J. M. Dent, 1907

Salinger, J. D., *Catcher in the Rye*, Hamish Hamilton, 1951

Segal, Muriel, *Virgins, Reluctant, Dubious and Avowed*, Robert Hale, 1978

Selye, Dr Hans, *Stress Without Distress*, Corgi, 1987 (New Ed. Pbk)

Simenon, Georges, *Intimate Memoirs*, Hamish Hamilton, 1984

Simons, G. L., *A History of Sex*, NEL, 1970

Solanis, Valerie, *Sisterhood is Powerful*, SCUM, New York, 1971

Strachey, Lytton, *Eminent Victorians*, Chatto and Windus, 1918

Tannahill, Reay, *Sex in History*, Hamish Hamilton, 1980

Taylor, G. Rattray, *Sex in History*, Thames and Hudson, 1959

Tripp, Rhoda Thomas, *The International Thesaurus of Quotations*, New York, 1970

Turner, E. S., *A History of Courting*, Michael Joseph, 1977

Wallace, Irving, Wallace, Amy, Walleschinsky, David and Wallace, Sylvia, *The Intimate Sex Lives of Famous People*, Hutchinson, 1982

Warhol, Andy, *From A. to B. and Back Again*, Cassell, 1975

Wells, G. P. (Ed.), *H. G. Wells in Love*, Faber and Faber, 1984

Wheat, Ed. M. D. and Wheat, Gaye, *Intended for Pleasure: Sex Technique and Sexual Fulfilment in Christian Marriage*, Scripture Union, 1979

Williams, Kenneth, *Just Williams: An Autobiography*, J. M. Dent, 1985

Wilson, Colin, *The Misfits*, Grafton Press, 1988

Wollard, Mrs E. O. G., *Sexology and the Philosophy of Life*, J. R. Walsh, Chicago, 1867